ANDREW MARTIN

Interior Design Review

Volume 9

ANDREW MARTIN
INTERNATIONAL

Martin Waller

Belinda Buckley

Editor: Martin Waller
Text: Belinda Buckley
Project Executive: Annika Bowman
Product Design: Graphicom Design

First Published in 2005 by Andrew Martin International

ISBN 0-9530045-7-0

Reproduction by Lamplight Group.
Printed in Singapore by Craft Print International Ltd.

Acknowledgments

The authors and publisher wish to thank all the owners and
designers of the projects featured in this book.

They also thank the following photographers:

Philip Vile, Vicente Wolf, Pere Planells, Dale Shiers, Edina
van der Wyck, Roland Roques-O'neil, Marco Ricca, Kate
Ayrton, William Abranowicz, Billy Cunningham, Scott
Frances, Jenny Acheson, Emanuel Bloedt, Claude-Simone
Langlois, Daniel Aubry, Mikhail Stepanov, Henry Bourne and
Simon Upton, Joseph Sy, Cees Roelofs, Brian Benson, Marc
Hertrich, Nicolas Adnet, Dook, David Ross-photos of
Westcliff house courtesy of Elle Décor SA, Michael Poliza,
Mickey Hoyle- courtesy of Elle Décor S. Africa, Costa
Economeades, House Design, Zeus of Hollywood, Bret
Casady, Tim Beddow, Mario Pignata Monti, Agi Simoes,
Patrick Tyberghein, Andreas von Einsiedel, Patrik Rytikangas
and Marco Ricca, David Garcia, Fritz von der Schulenburg,
Michael Stepanov, Eugene Liberov, Peter Harrison, Peter
Kooijman Photography, Ali Bekman, Reha Ercan, Levent
Bozkurt, Seyhan Özdemir, Sefer Çaglar, Bahadir Tanriover,
Roberto Battistini, Jean-Marc Palisse, David O. Marlow,
Vangelis Paterakis, Baily Chan, George Apostolidis, Daniel
Aubry, Nikolas Koenig, Durston Saylor, Michael Jäckel,
Richard Waite, Thibault Jeanson, Wouter van der Toe, Peter
Murdock, Andreas Einsiedel, Dennis Krukowski, David
Churchill, Simon Rowell, Dickie Bannenberg, David Archer,
Benetti Yachts, Italy, Mr Steve Mok and Mr Ulso Tsang, Ted
Yardwood, Joy Vontiedemann, Modestas Ezerskis and
Narimantas Serksnys, James Balston and Adam Parker, Koray
Erkaya, John Kane, Ilya Babak, Michael Stepanov, Cyril
Ovchinnikov, Francis Smith, Dennis Krukowski, Giorgio
Baroni, Phil Conrad, Jeremy Kicks, Philip Bier, Thierry
Cardineau, Facundo de Zuviria, Mike Swartz Photography,
Francisco de Almeida Dias, Luke Forman, Ari Karttunen,
Warren Smith Photography.com, Daniela Rosenfeld, Ken
Kirkwood, Tim Soar of Soargallery, Richard Waite.com, Helen
Tschudi, Mona Gundersen, Christian Rochat, James
Mortimer, Grant Scott, J. Sierra and Cunard Line Limited,
Francoise de Pfyffer, Tim Beddow, Patricio Miguel, Chris
Tubbs, Richard Booth, Veronika Sittard, Craig Fraser and
Christian Diedericks, Beto Riginik, Romulo Fialdini, Hugo
Burnard, Jake Fitzjones, Viewpoint Photography Ltd.

The disappearance of national cultural identities
have become an accepted truism of recent
years. MTV, CNN, Friends, Manchester United,
are all omnipotent. In Vietnam David Beckham's
poster stares down from every billboard.

The more remarkable fact is how national
stereotypes are still so marked. Walking down
any major shopping street in any city in the
world, the same store brands dominate.
Nevertheless its still a cinch to recognise the
nationality of shoppers just by the way they
dress. Italians knot their ties differently,
Germans have a unique colour preference in
jackets, the French stick to a timeless
classicism, Americans have a love affair with
sneakers and chinos.

The same is true in interiors. It may be that all
the major furniture and fabric houses sell in
every market, but how designers in each country
use these products remains utterly different.

The French colour palette is theirs alone. A
mauve and green combo is a regular standby
rather than the occasional indulgence.

Italy's long love affair with modernism is well
documented as is the distinctive Scandinavian
mix of 20th century classic with comfort and
warmth.

In the Far East the same obsession that makes
their cities such spectacular night time viewing
ensures that lighting is not just a facilitator but
actually the rasion d'etre of a scheme.

American interiors are singled out by a vigorous
precision. Even in casual locations at country or
beach houses the furniture layouts and colour
schemes are executed with considered
exactitude.

By contrast in the UK, its considered bad
manners to be seen to be trying too hard.
Consequently designers strive to make their role
invisible. The supreme achievement is when a
house looks as if it was last decorated 50 years
before.

Such is the complex background to the rapids
that must be navigated every year by the judges
at the International Design Awards. This years
volume of the Andrew Martin Design Review
underlines just how difficult it is.

MARTIN WALLER

Tara B

ernerd

DESIGNER: TARA BERNERD
COMPANY: TARGET LIVING, LONDON, ENGLAND

Projects: Houses and apartments in large luxury
residential developments, commercial commissions
for spaces such as art galleries. Has just launched
her own line of furniture

FANTASY COVER STORY: PLAYBOY 'INTERIOR DESIGNER OF THE YEAR'

Would like to have been floating there when Neil Armstong planted that flag

Fascinated by the KGB

Wishes cigarettes had never been invented

Wants to be Princess Leia in Star Wars "It's a Jedi thing"

Would like to be sculpted by Duane Hanson

Collects art and wants a Basquiat

Could live forever in the Popollo suite with the adjoining room 608 as her bedroom in the Hotel de Russie, Rome

If all she could furnish a house with was a phone, she'd be right on it to order more stuff, particularly a Philippe Starck day bed

'IT SOUNDS EASIER THAN IT IS, BUT 'BE YOURSELF' IS THE BEST PIECE OF ADVICE TO ANYONE'

Projects: High end residential interiors, commercial and public buildings around the USA

Vicente Wolf

Designer: Vicente Wolf. Company: Vicente Wolf Associates, New York, USA. Didn't do well in school. Was exiled from Cuba. Wants to work for Nelson Mandela. Would have loved to have been Phileas Fogg or Fred Astaire in Funny Face. Wishes to be cremated and have his ashes scattered in the Himalayas.

Fantasy cover story: Time, 'Evolving designer.'

'IT'S IMPORTANT TO CREATE AN ENVIRONMENT THAT DOESN'T STRAY FROM THE EMOTION OF THE PLACE'

Projects: Residences, restaurants and hotels across Spain, London and Moscow

Jorge Fuentes

Designer: Jorge Fuentes. Company: Studio F Interiors, Barcelona, Spain. Wishes he were an artist. Wants Castro to be retired. Covets Van Gogh's Sunflowers. Wishes Gaudi could design him a house in Barcelona. That he could paint taupe. And furnish with a Galuchat cabinet by Jean-Michel Frank. Would die happy if he could see Brad Pitt naked. Fantasy cover story: Time, 'Designer of the Year.'

'I DON'T LIKE GETTING STUCK IN ONE KIND OF MOTIF'

Projects: Contemporary residences and luxury ski chalets

Designer: Nicky Dobree. Company: Nicky Dobree Interior Design, London, England. Would liked to have been a dancer. Wants to shop forever in Henri Bendel, New York. Wants to be sculpted by Sean Henry. Would like to be Elastigirl from The Incredibles. Her dream is to live in a house on a cliff overlooking the sea, designed by Norwegian architect Henriette Salvesen. Likes the idea of a party in a Bedouin tent in the midst of the Sahara.

Fantasy cover story: Grand Designs magazine,

'Chalet chic.'

Nicky Dobree

'I DO WISH PEOPLE
WOULD NOT HAVE A
FEAR OF QUALITY'

Projects: Residential and hospitality design, including the Four Seasons and Savoy Group plus the offices of a Head of State

Designer: Alexandra Champalimaud. Company: Alexandra Champalimaud & Associates, New York, Montreal, Los Angeles and London. Wishes she could have seen Eve eating the apple. Would like to rid the world of religious persecution. Dreams of being a great Fado singer. Wishes she could join the order of the Knights of Malta. Would shop till she dropped at Christie's. Wishes she could have sat for Frances Bacon. Left Portugal with her two sons and a jewellery box.

Alexandra
Champalimaud

'I BELIEVE IN TRANSFORMING SPACES, TO FIND
FIVE STAR LUXURY IN UNEXPECTED PLACES'

DESIGNER: IRINA DYMOVA
COMPANY: IRINA DYMOVA DESIGN STUDIO,
MOSCOW, RUSSIA

Irina Dymova

Projects: High-end private residences and some commercial property

Trained in journalism. Thinks being 40 is fabulous. Collects men. Loathes hospitals. Would splurge at the Sanderson Hotel in London. But fancies being interred in Red Square.

Kit Kemp

**DESIGNER:
KIT KEMP
COMPANY:
FIRMDALE HOTELS,
LONDON, ENGLAND**

**Projects:
Townhouse
hotels, bars,
restaurants,
& occasional
residential
projects**

Originally wanted to be a dressage rider

Would love to be speaker of the House of Commons

Could die happy shopping at De Beers

Thinks the motor industry needs to use more chrome

Utterly loves Bewitched - wishes she could be Samantha

Runs marathons

Collects stones with holes

'THERE ARE SO MANY PASTICHE HIP HOTELS THAT ARE TOO MUCH OF A FORMULA. IT'S NOT ABOUT FASHION IT'S ABOUT HAVING A HEART'

FANTASY
COVER STORY:
VOGUE
'WHAT WRINKLES?'

'YOU'VE GOT TO WORK ON DETAIL ALL THE TIME. AND YOU'VE GOT TO BE ABLE TO ADD TO THAT DETAIL A FEW YEARS DOWN THE LINE'

Joseph

DESIGNER: JOSEPH SY
COMPANY: JOSEPH SY & ASSOCIATES,
HONG KONG

Sy

思妍丽
—— Health & Beauty SPA ——

8
SOHO
别墅 Villa

Projects: Restaurants, shops and residences in Hong Kong, China, The Philippines and England

A pen represents his personality. Wants to be the Pink Panther. Is exhausted by Hong Kong's horrendous traffic. Would love to rid politics of corrupt officials.

FANTASY COVER STORY: LIFE 'ARTIST OF THE MONTH'

Jan des

DESIGNER: JAN DES BOUVRIE
COMPANY: STUDIO HET ARSENAAL,
NAARDEN, HOLLAND

56

Bouvrie

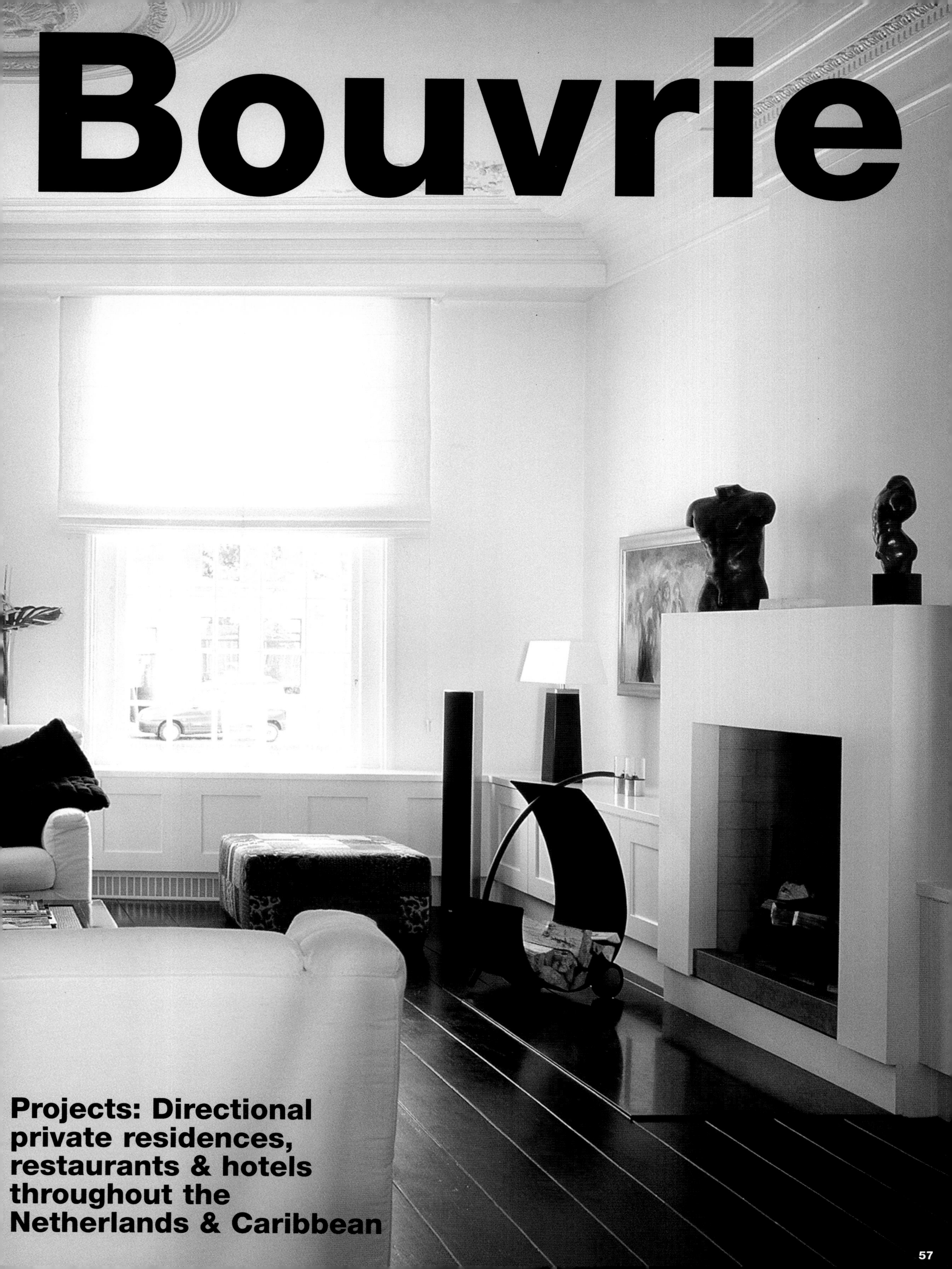

**Projects: Directional
private residences,
restaurants & hotels
throughout the
Netherlands & Caribbean**

Dyslexic. Loves the timelessness of the Chanel logo. Despises forgeries. Wishes he could be painted by Andy Warhol. Or to have lived in Amsterdam during Holland's Golden age (1600s). Craves a collection of work by Gilbert and George. Enjoys the view from his office window.

FANTASY COVER STORY: WALLPAPER 'SIMPLICITY'

DESIGNER: RABIH HAGE
COMPANY: RABIH HAGE LTD,
LONDON, ENGLAND

Rabih Hage

Would be a student again at Villa Medici in Rome. Yet yearns to be a professional yachtsman. Economy class in aeroplanes should never have been considered. Compares himself to a Rubik's Cube with seven colours, not six. Collects cigars. Could paint his whole world aubergine. Wants to go into Space and look down at the Earth and be buried on the moon. Dying to throw a party in the Oval Office of the White House.

Fantasy cover story: GQ, 'Unbelievable weight loss.'

Projects: Mostly residential in Britain and France, some commercial work and furniture design

'IF YOU ONLY HAVE ONE PIECE OF FURNITURE, MAKE IT MY COCOON DAYBED. THIS PIECE IS MULTI-FUNCTIONAL , IT CAN BE AS A BED AND A SOFA, EITHER ON YOUR OWN OR WITH OTHER PEOPLE'

DESIGNERS: MARC HERTRICH & NICOLAS ADNET
COMPANY: STUDIO MARC HERTRICH,
PARIS, FRANCE

Nicolas Adnet

Projects: Private residences, hotels, restaurants, social and commercial property

Both wish they had been to Paris' Great Exhibition of 1900. Want to attend St Martin's School of Art in London. Or be psychoanalysts. A television was their worst purchase. Yet they think Absolutely Fabulous is brilliant. Would be painted by Balthus.

FANTASY COVER STORY: CITIZEN K (HIP PARISIAN FASHION MAGAZINE) 'DESIGNERS WITH CONSCIENCE'

'WHEN WORKING ON HOTELS OR RESTAURANTS,

'GIVE FULL REIGN TO OUR SENSE OF CONVIVIALITY'

Projects: Low environmental impact, luxury lodges, resorts and residences across southern Africa and the Seychelles

Silvio Rech

Believes in stylish travel, stylishly designed. Would like to be a member of the Ferrari Club in Modena, Italy. Would enrol right now at Venice Architecture School. Wishes he could have been around at the height of Beatlemania - as a Beatle. As Minister of Arts, he would ensure the style police were active. His dream house would be designed by Ron Arad on top of Battersea Power Station.

Fantasy cover story: Domus magazine, 'so that my relatives could see it.'

'Italian trailblazer in South Africa.'

DESIGNER: SILVIO RECH
COMPANY: SILVIO RECH & LESLEY CARSTENS
ARCHITECTURE & INTERIOR DESIGN,
JOHANNESBURG, SOUTH AFRICA

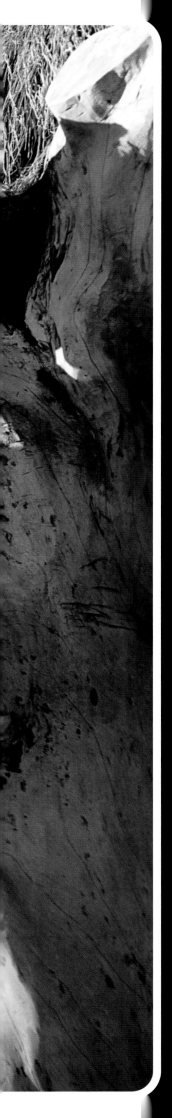

'I LOVE THE ITALIAN DESIGN ETHIC, THAT IT MUST HAVE EMOTION'

Frederick

Frederick

DESIGNER: FREDERICK SUTHERLAND
COMPANY: FREDERICK SUTHERLAND
& CO, VENICE, CALIFORNIA, USA

Sutherland

Projects:
Boutique hotels, bars, clubs,
art galleries and contemporary
residences around California

**FANTASY COVER STORY:
TIME
'THE FACE OF THE CURE
FOR CANCER'**

Hated school

Would have liked to have been a cartoonist

Wishes he had designed the Coca-Cola logo

Best thing he ever bought was his wife's wedding ring

Thunderbirds is the best television show ever

Will always live in Venice, California

Collects Venetian glass

And would like to be a space tourist

'THESE ARE THE GOOD OLD DAYS,
SO WHY GO BACK IN TIME?'

Artistic

DESIGNER: DMITRY VELIKOVSKY
COMPANY: ARTISTIC DESIGN, MOSCOW, RUSSIA

Design

Projects: Contemporary high end residential

FANTASY COVER STORY: NATIONAL GEOGRAPHIC 'LOST TRIBE'

'I'D LOVE TO TELL THE AUTOMOBILE INDUSTRY TO LOOK TO DESIGNS OF THE PAST'

Would like to be a Freemason

Shops till he drops in the antique shops of Kathmandu

Yet is a modernist at heart

Buys art by Columbian Fernando Botero

Favourite work of art: Uccello's battle scene in London's National Gallery

Would commission Richard Neutra to build his dream home in Gambia

Best hotel Neemrana Fort-Palace Hotel in Rajasthan

Sara Al-Faisal

Designer: Sara Al Faisal. Company: Sima Malak & Alssamoure Design Associates, Riyadh, Saudi Arabia. History buff. Could have been a carpenter. Wishes she could have been painted by Michelangelo. Loves the Mercer Hotel. Wants to be buried in Medina.

Fantasy cover story: Would never appear on the cover of a magazine, unless it could be as a silhouette of her profile, with the caption: 'Unidentified Saudi woman accidentally finds cure for all cancers by mixing plants in her garden.'

Projects: Luxury residences, royal palaces, urban apartments and country estates, commercial property in the Middle East, Europe and the USA

'I BELIEVE I PROVIDE CLIENTS WITH A FRESH ALTERNATIVE TO THE STEREOTYPICAL, TRADITIONAL IDEAL OF OPULENCE GENERALLY FOUND WITHIN THIS REGION'

**Projects:
Mainly
residential,
some
commercial**

Sue
Rohrer

Designer: Sue Rohrer. Company Sue Rohrer

Zumikon, Zurich, Switzerland. Wants to

study at St Martin's School of Art, London.

Could be exiled with just her Amex card.

Would paint her whole house black. Feels

that cars should run on alternative energy.

Would love to be painted by Modigliani.

Covets an Alexander Calder mobile. Wants to

do lunch with Karl Largerfeld.

Fantasy cover story: Financial Times'

How To Spend It magazine,

'Biggest Lottery Winner, ever.'

'I WOULD LOVE TO ASK PHILIPPE STARCK TO BUILD ME A HOME IN LONDON'

Carter**ty**

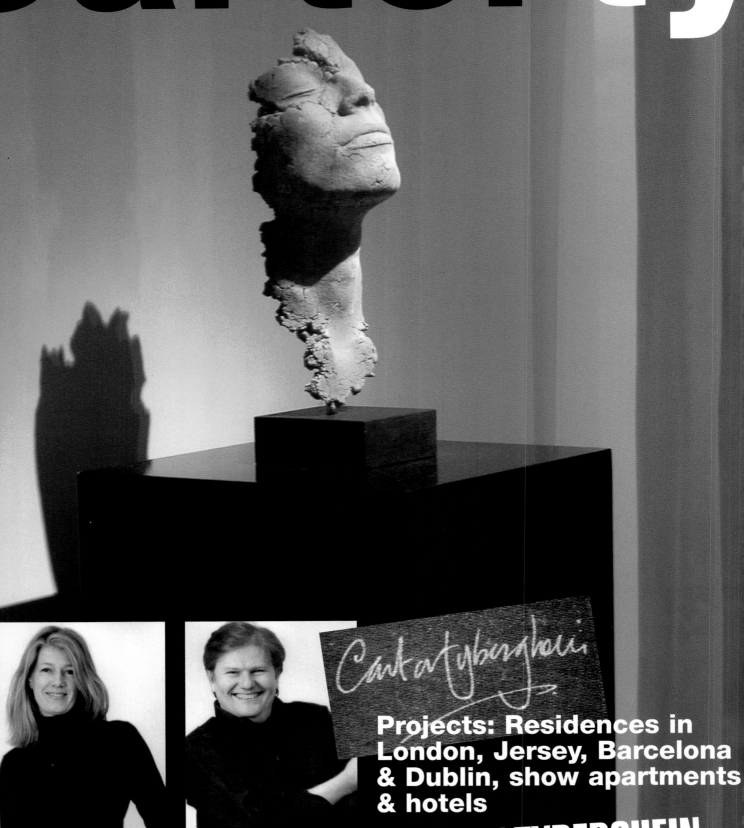

Cartertyberghein

Projects: Residences in London, Jersey, Barcelona & Dublin, show apartments & hotels

DESIGNERS: LAURA CARTER & PATRICK TYBERGHEIN
COMPANY: CARTERTYBERGHEIN, LONDON, ENGLAND

berghein

Patrick gets reminded weekly that England defeated the French at Agincourt

They'd like to enroll at Harvard

Laura fancied being a barrister; Patrick, an artist

Laura would happily be Lauren Hutton in American Gigolo

But she identifies with Austen's Jane Bennett from Pride and Prejudice

Crave a holiday house by the sea with sandy beaches, such as on Cape Verde

And the dream would be to have Tandao Ando build it

Never want to be buried

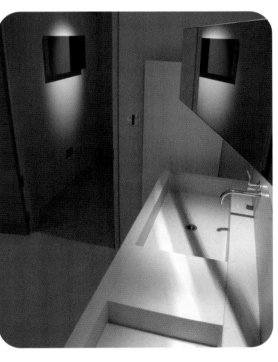

'A WARMER, MORE HUMAN APPROACH WILL COME INTO CONTEMPORARY INTERIORS'

Projects: Town and country residences across Northern Europe

Peter Nolden

Designer: Peter Nolden. Company: Peter Nolden Interior Design, Hamburg, Germany. Would have loved to have discovered Tutankhamen's tomb. Could spend the rest of his days shopping at Axel Vervoordt in Antwerp. Believes that Benetton's 'Multiracial' campaign was the best. Wishes plastic had never been invented. Compares himself to a pair of John Lobb shoes.

Fantasy cover story: German Architectural Digest, 'Simply the best.'

'APPARENTLY, I AM A MAN OF THE 18TH CENTURY. BUT WHILE I MIGHT LIKE THE DESIGNS OF THAT ERA, I DO WANT THEM TO BE COMBINED WITH MODERN DAY FUNCTIONALITY: I MEAN, THE MOST IMPORTANT INVENTION IN HISTORY WAS ELECTRIC LIGHT'

Projects: Classic contemporary American style homes and beach houses in New York, the Hamptons and Florida

Scott Sanders

Would have liked to have gone to the Black and White Ball at the Plaza Hotel thrown by Truman Capote in 1966. Would like to be Head of Design for Steve Wynn, the Las Vegas property magnate. The Brady Bunch was the best TV show. Would have a home in Knightsbridge, London and a holiday house on Lake Como, Italy. But would like his bedroom to be room 221 of the Hotel Splendido in Portofino, overlooking the Italian Riviera. His dream home would be in Southport Connecticut and constructed by the 19th century New England firm of architects McKim, Mead and White.

Fantasy cover story: New York magazine,

'NY designer chosen to redecorate the White House.'

DESIGNER: SCOTT SANDERS
COMPANY: SCOTT SANDERS LLC,
NEW YORK CITY, USA

FANCIES COLLECTING MERCEDES CONVERTABLES: 'I NEVER SAW ONE I DIDN'T LOVE'

'NEVER EVER BURN BRIDGES'

Jane Churchill

Designer: Jane Churchill. Company: Jane Churchill Interiors, London, England. Thinks the Mile High Club sounds more entertaining than Brownies. Would buy everything possible in Neiman Marcus, Dallas, Texas. Desperate Housewives is the best TV show ever. Everything goes with French Grey. Wants a view of English parkland with deer. Fantasises about Hawksmoor building her a house in a warm climate.

Fantasy cover story: Time magazine, 'Discoverer of a cure for all cancer.'

Projects: Residential properties and executive offices

'I WOULD LIKE TO REMOVE THE MODERN PREJUDICE THAT DISCIPLINE IS A BAD THING'

'I COLLECT CANDLESTICKS, AS I HAVE A LIBERACE FETISH AND WE ALL LOOK BETTER BY CANDLELIGHT'

Nadya A

DESIGNER: NADYA ANANIEVA
COMPANY: NADYA AND GEORGY ANANIEV
INTERIOR DESIGN AND ARCHITECTURE

Projects: Private apartments, beauty salons, bars, cafes, multifunctional recreation centres and a casino

FANTASY COVER STORY: NEW SCIENTIST 'SHE BROKE THE LAW OF GRAVITY TO LET EVERYONE FLY'

Could have been a professional dancer

Would thrash her plastic in Prada

Believes the invention of mirror coating had historic impact

And that cars should have their interiors upholstered orange

Would have loved to have lived the life of Anna Karenina

Wants everyone to get over the prejudice that all blondes are dumb

Projects: Elaborate big events for leading corporations and media show houses

David Lees

Designer: David Lees. Company: David Lees Productions, New York, USA. Worked at Studio 54. Would love to study music at Juilliard. Would like to work for Steven Spielberg. Wishes chewing gum had never been invented. Fancies being United States Ambassador to Japan. And to go shopping with Elton John in London. Could live with just a 1912 Steinway Grand Piano. Would be buried in the Pyramid at Giza.

Fantasy cover story: New York magazine, 'David Lees - corporate America's secret promotional design weapon.'

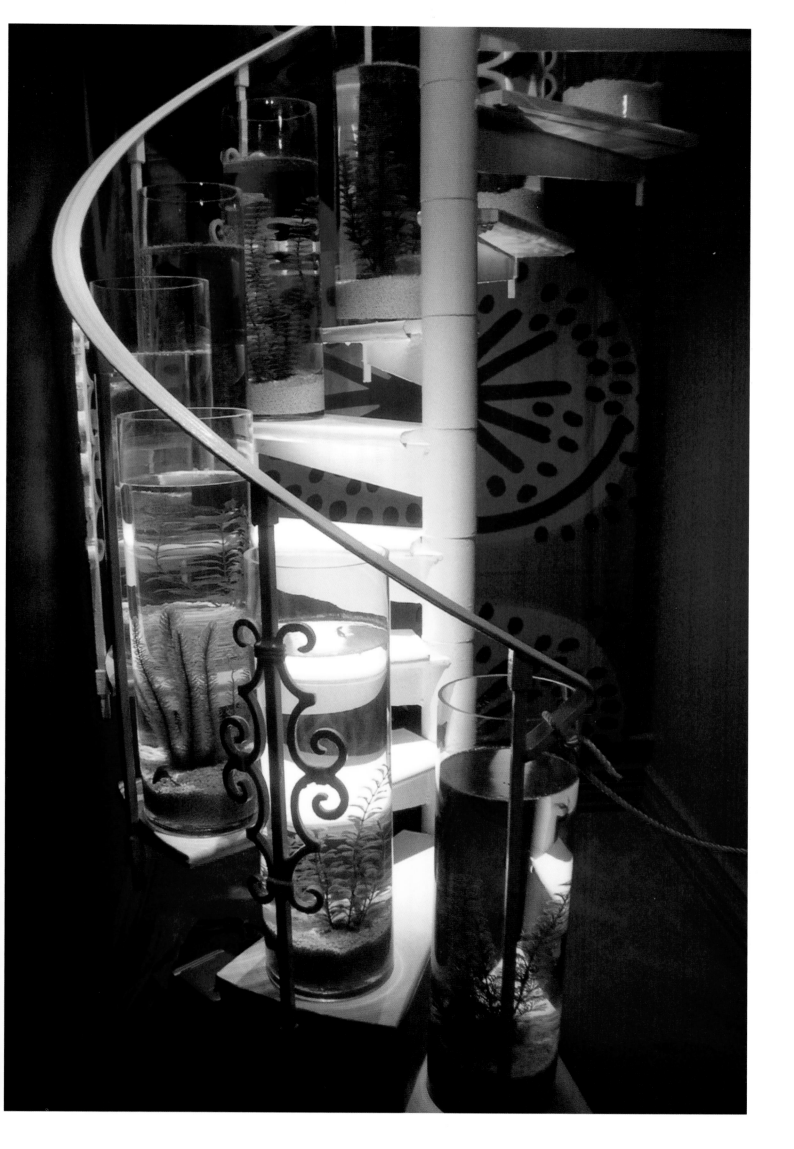

'GREAT LIGHTING ENHANCES EVERYTHING'

DESIGNERS: OSCA & PIERRETTE REUCHLIN
COMPANY: GR HOME, BLOEMENDAAL, HOLLAND

Osca &
Pierrette
Reuchlin

**Projects:
Private town
& country
residences
around the
Netherlands**

Sisters. Wish they'd witnessed the invention of chocolate. Both could shop till they dropped in any of Etro's stores. And think Absolut's advertising has become art. And wine that gives you headaches - chateau migraine - should be abolished. Both love their typical Dutch canal house and its view of the canals. But they'd have Rem Koolhaas design them a house in London if they could. They'd throw a glittering do in Baccarat's Crystal Room in Paris, designed by Philippe Starck.

We like to incorporate customers' collected furniture into coherent contemporary settings

Seyhan Özdemir & Sefer Çaglar

DESIGNERS: SEYHAN OZDEMIR & SEFER CAGLAR COMPANY: AUTOBAN DESIGN STUDIO, ISTANBUL, TURKEY

Projects: Restaurants, boutiques, bars and cafes, country houses and loft apartments

He wants a holiday home in Malibu. She wants one on Koh Phi Phi

He collects lamps. She collects sunglasses

Seyhan's party venue the Barcelona Pavillion by Mies Van Der Rohe

Sefer's having a bash in the harem at the Topkapi Palace

Both would spoil themselves rotten at Soho House, New York

Fantasy cover stories:

Sehan: National Geographic, 'A regular person.'

Sefer: Time, 'Untitled.'

'WE LIKE STRONG USE OF NATURAL MATERIALS WITH A CONTRASTING INDUSTRIAL APPROACH'

DESIGNER: FRANÇOIS CHAMPSAUR
COMPANY: AGENCE FRANÇOIS CHAMPSAUR, PARIS, FRANCE

HAMPSAUR

Projects: Apartments, town and country houses, boutique hotels and high end restaurants

Wishes he'd lived in Pompeii. Likes photographic art. Thinks Paris Hilton should be herself. Is keen to visit the savannah of Africa. Would have a Gehry designed house on the US west coast.

'I DON'T EVER WANT TO FIND MYSELF ON THE FIRST PAGE OR COVER OF ANY MAGAZINE'

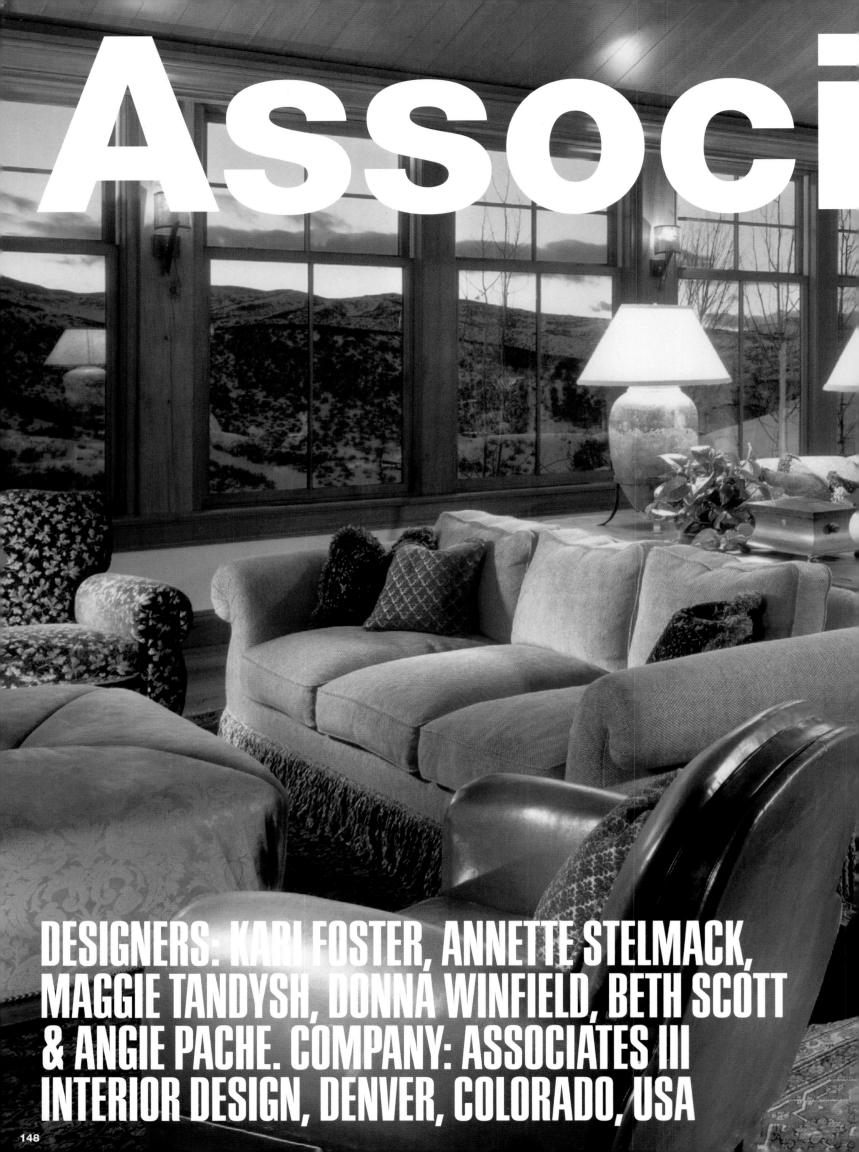

Associ

DESIGNERS: KARI FOSTER, ANNETTE STELMACK, MAGGIE TANDYSH, DONNA WINFIELD, BETH SCOTT & ANGIE PACHE. COMPANY: ASSOCIATES III INTERIOR DESIGN, DENVER, COLORADO, USA

ates III

Projects:
Contemporary luxurious private residences, commercial & hospitality properties with low environmental impact worldwide

Members of the National Resource Defence council and the Heifer Foundation

Could probably live in the Tattered Cover bookstore in Denver

Wish that PVC had never been invented

Want to be Secretary of the Interior to the US Government

Would throw a casual drinks do at sunset on a warm summer evening atop Machu Picchu, after hiking all day

Want their ashes scattered on a lake overlooking Pikes Peak, Colorado

'STRONG, COMPASSIONATE WOMEN WHO INSPIRE CHANGE TOWARD A HEALTHIER ENVIRONMENT FOR ALL'

Projects:
Contemporary residences and boutique hotels in Greece, Istanbul, Cyprus and New York

Angelos Angelopoulos

Designer: Angelos Angelopoulos. Company: Angelos Angelopoulos Interior Design, Athens, Greece. Hermes is a diachronic logo of the past century. Would liked to have worked for Mother Teresa as a missionary. Adores The Muppet Show. Collects watches. Covets anything by MC Escher. Wishes to be cremated and scattered in the Aegean Sea.

Fantasy cover story: The New Yorker,

'He is making the world more beautiful.'

'MY NEW BOHEMIAN STYLE IS ALL FLASHY SUMMER COLOURS, FLORAL COMPOSITIONS, SEVENTIES BOLSTERS, VINTAGE ELEMENTS AND CRYSTAL CHANDELIERS'

Law Ling Kit & Virginia Lung

**Projects:
Show apartments, high end
residences and club houses in
Hong Kong, China and Singapore**

Both believe that the Nanjing Massacre was China's darkest moment. Kit wishes he'd coined the Louis Vuitton logo; Virginia the Olympic rings. Kit likes a view facing a pretty girl's home. Virginia prefers Hong Kong's harbour. Kit collects design books. Virginia would sit for Monet if she could.

Fantasy cover story: Times Magazine, 'Cool eastern interior design.'

'WHAT WE WANT IS TO CREATE A CHINESE STYLE, DIFFERENT FROM TRADITION AND EXPECTATION'

Projects: Luxury hotels for prominent hospitality corporations around the world

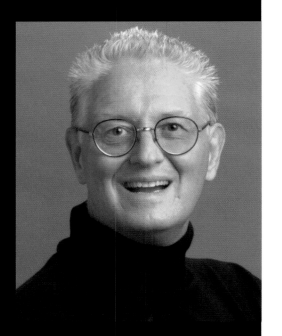

Michael Bedner

Designer: Michael Bedner. Company: Hirsch Bedner Associates, Los Angeles, USA. Being a wild-assed liberal, is a fan of the West Wing. Would choose Alan Bate's role in the film of DH Lawrence's Women in Love for himself. Would revere any piece by Mark Rothko. Would paint a whole house Heavy Hampshire Cream. Collects Inuit art.

'WE WORK TO CREATE FANTASY, PROVIDE COMFORT AND ADD A SENSE OF DRAMA AND THEATRE - A STAGE FOR GUEST'S EXPERIENCE A ACTOR AND AUDIENCE'

'I'M PROUD THAT HBA HAS BEEN KNOWN AS THE 'GRADUATE SCHOOL' FOR THE HOSPITALITY DESIGN INDUSTRY AND THAT WE HAVE HELPED DEVELOP SO MUCH TALENT IN OUR INDUSTRY'

Toni E

DESIGNER: TONI ESPUCH
COMPANY: AZUL TIERRA, ALICANTE, SPAIN

Projects: Country houses, penthouses, lofts, ships, restaurants, offices and shops around Spain

spuch

Entirely self-taught. Never had a job interview. Wishes he'd lived in ancient Egypt. Wants to star in My Life Without Me. Collects Roman sculpture. But won't sit for any artist. Is a bit of a Peter Pan. Dying to go to Madagascar. Wants to hang out at Hotel Begawan Giri, Bali.

'I CREATE A WORLD WHERE (

SMOPOLITAN MEETS ETHNIC'

Projects: Contemporary residences and hotels in London and the Caribbean

Helen Green

Designer: Helen Green. Company: Helen Green Design, London, England. Wishes she'd been at the Great Exhibition at Crystal Palace, London in 1851. Loves the Chanel logo. Spray paint should never have been invented, 'it's only blighted the delights of urban living.' Craves a Park Avenue penthouse. But only needs a Mallorcan finca to holiday in.

Fantasy cover story: Vanity Fair,

'Green - the new black.'

'PEOPLE WANT AN ECLECTIC MIX OF FURNITURE NOW. THEY ARE AFTER CAREFULLY CHOSEN ANTIQUES, RATHER THAN EVERYTHING BRAND NEW FROM A STATE OF THE ART FURNITURE STORE'

Alessand

DESIGNER:
ALESSANDRA BRANCA
COMPANY:
BRANCA, CHICAGO,
ILLINOIS, USA

a Branca

Projects: Classic American luxury residences

Thanks—
call me
w/questions!
Anne

BRANCA

Anne Monoky

1325 North State Parkway | Chicago, Illinois 60610 USA
tele.312.787.6123 | fax.312.787.6125 | amonoky@branca.com

FANTASY COVER STORY: PARENTS MAGAZINE 'WE SURVIVED TEENAGERS'

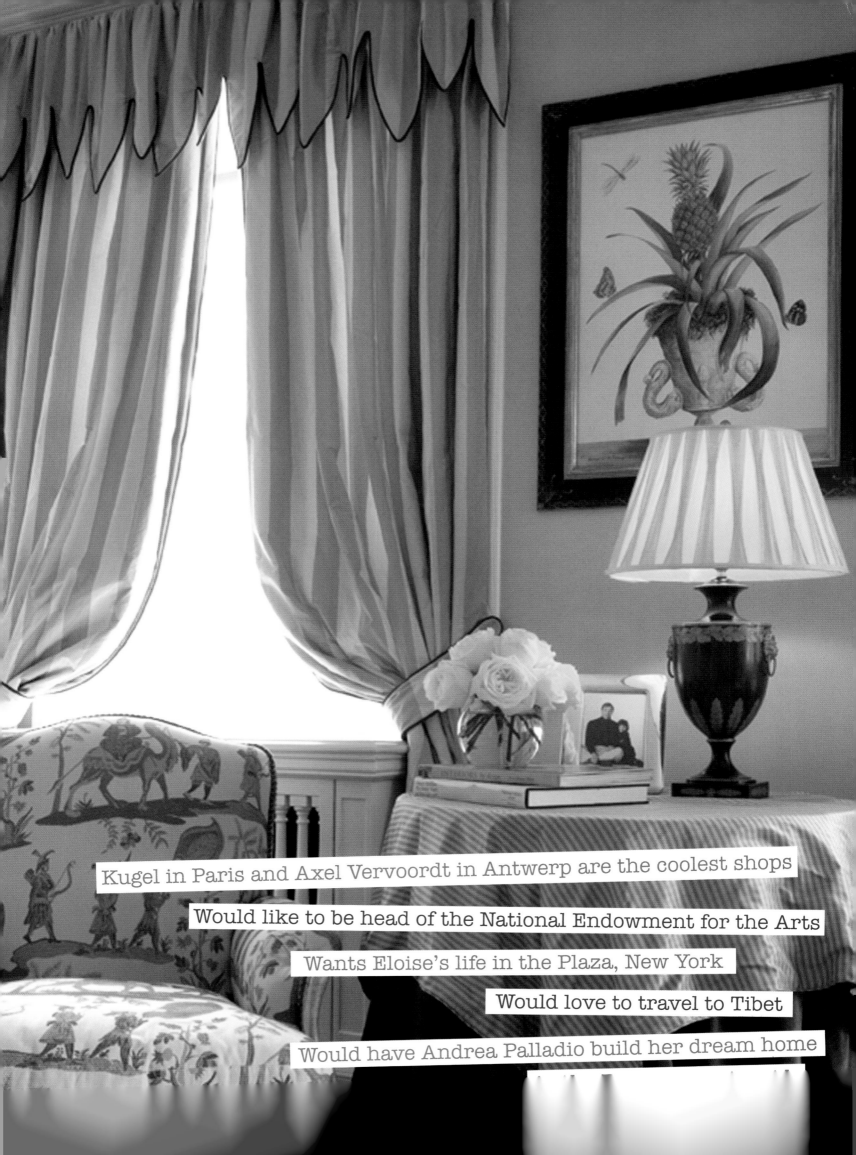

Kugel in Paris and Axel Vervoordt in Antwerp are the coolest shops

Would like to be head of the National Endowment for the Arts

Wants Eloise's life in the Plaza, New York

Would love to travel to Tibet

Would have Andrea Palladio build her dream home

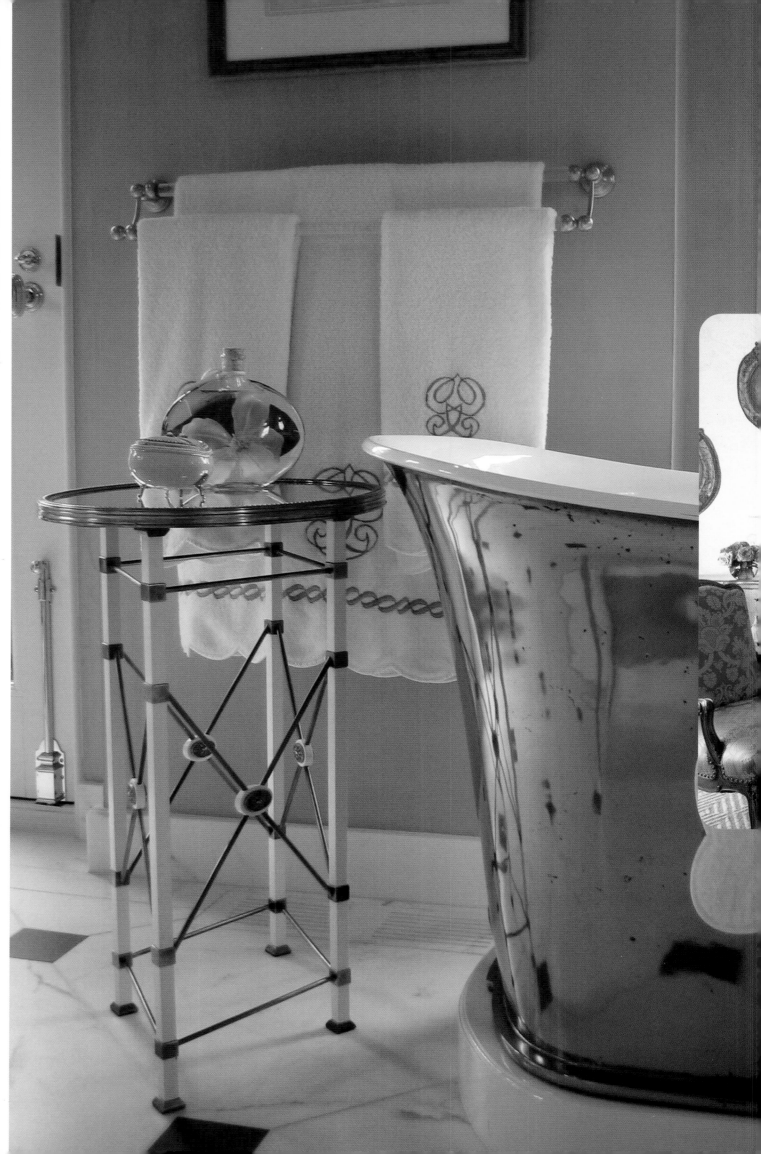

'I DON'T FOLLOW TRENDS – I RUN FROM THEM'

ALBERTO PINTO Classic

A HOUSE IS NOT A HOME Bruce Weber

'IF YOU ARE TRYING TO MAKE SOMETHING FOR LESS, MAKE IT G
ALWAYS INSULTING TO THE END USER...YOU ARE ALWAYS GO

FOR LESS. TO START AT THE HIGHEST LEVEL AND DUMBDOWN IS O LOSE THAT THING THAT MADE IT SPECIAL TO START WITH'

Ernest de la Torre

Designer: Ernest de la Torre. Company: de la Torre design studio, New York, USA. Would be apprentice to Frank Gehry. Wishes gunpowder and polyester had never been invented. Thinks South Park is the cleverest TV show. Wants to sit for Lucian Freud. Covets Picasso's Guernica. Wants his ashes thrown to the sea from St Bart's at Pointe Milou, 'so I could be in the warm sun forever.' Wishes Le Corbusier could build him a glass house in Big Sur. Fantasy cover story: W magazine, 'Top designer tapped for White House renovation.'

Projects: Classic contemporary urban and country luxury residences in the US and the UK

'I'D LOVE TO CALL UP PARIS HILTON AND TELL HER 'SLOW DOWN ON THE RHINESTONES!'

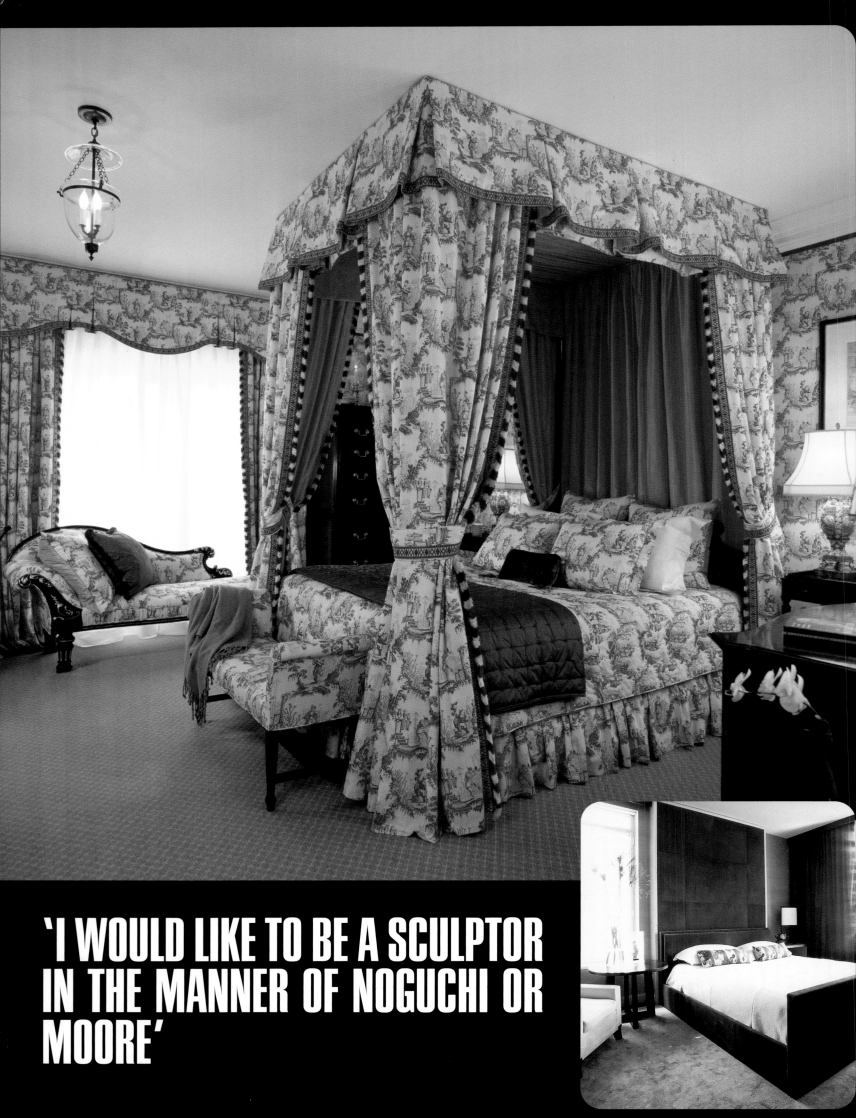

'I WOULD LIKE TO BE A SCULPTOR IN THE MANNER OF NOGUCHI OR MOORE'

DESIGNER: DICKIE BANNENBERG
COMPANY: JON BANNENBERG LTD, LONDON, ENGLAND

**Projects:
Luxury
cruisers and
superyachts**

nnenberg

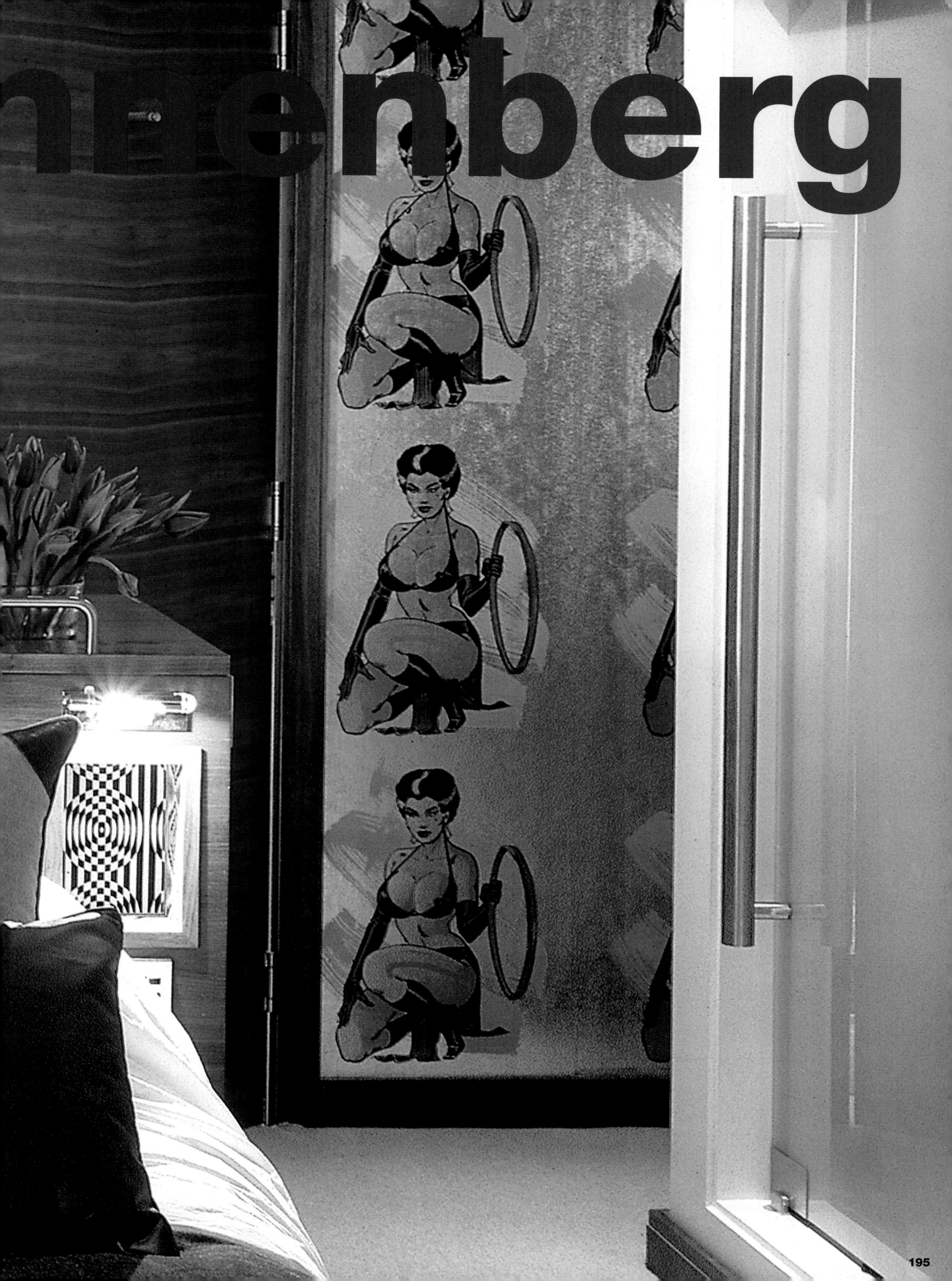

FANTASY COVER STORY: FINANCIAL TIMES' HOW TO SPEND IT MAGAZINE 'WHY YOU MUST DO YOUR YACHT WITH THIS MAN'

Loves the aesthetics of the London Underground logo

Spends heavily on the iTunes website

Would work as a Polaroid warmer for Annie Leibovitz if he could

Chewing gum should never have been invented

Wants to be Michael Caine in The Italian Job

Or to be a sculpture by Barry Flanagan

Would like to collect Fiat 500s. Currently only collects parking tickets

'THE MOST VALUABLE PIECE OF ADVICE I'VE HAD WAS FROM MY FATHER JON BANNENBERG; 'THERE ARE SO MANY SOLUTIONS''

Projects: Minimalist modern houses, apartments, clubs and restaurants in China

Steve Leung

Designer: Steve Leung. Company: Steve Leung Designers, Hong Kong. Ardent advocate of minimalism. Collects nothing. Doesn't care for shopping. Adores his mother country and home town of Hong Kong. Wishes he could have lived during the Tang Dynasty. Could paint his entire home light grey and live with just a Corbusier chaise longue.

Fantasy cover story: Wallpaper, 'Chinese minimalism.'

'THERE'S AN OLD CHINESE SAYING THAT A CONTENTED MIND IS A PERPETUAL FEAST'

'MY WORK REFLECTS A STRONG AND UNIQUE CHARACTER OF MINIMALISM WITH ADOPTION OF ASIAN CULTURE AND ARTS'

Projects: Up-scale private residences, hotels and country clubs across the Americas

Brian Gluckstein

Designer: Brian Gluckstein. Company: Gluckstein Design Planning, Toronto, Canada. Would like to live in London, with a holiday house on Lake Como, built by Palladio. Could paint his house ivory throughout. And have a great four poster bed as his sole piece of furniture. Would be painted by Caravaggio. Loves the Coke campaign, 'I'd like to teach the world to sing...'

Fantasy cover story: Time,

'Brian Gluckstein: making life better through design.'

Ricardas V

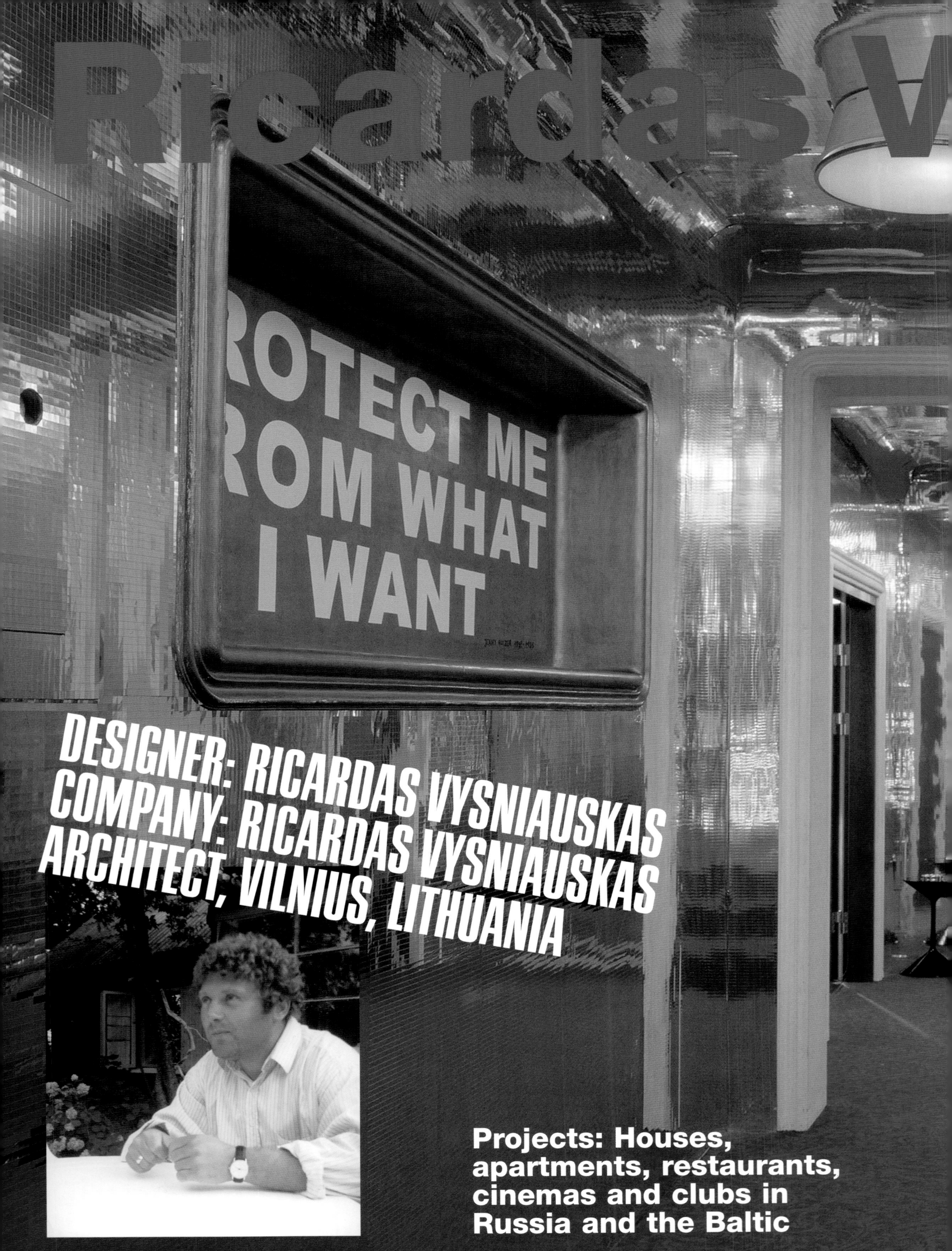

ROTECT ME
ROM WHAT
I WANT

DESIGNER: RICARDAS VYSNIAUSKAS
COMPANY: RICARDAS VYSNIAUSKAS ARCHITECT, VILNIUS, LITHUANIA

Projects: Houses, apartments, restaurants, cinemas and clubs in Russia and the Baltic

Has serious brand loyalty to Gucci

Would have loved to have been a forestry officer

Views politics as pointless

Has the temperament of mercury

Wants to go to the North Pole

'NEVER WANTS TO BE ON THE FRONT COVER OF A MAGAZINE'

Projects:
Up-market classic residential and commercial across Europe and the USA

Joanna Wood

Could happily have been a theatre set designer: 'it's the ultimate in styling.' Was once PA to the UN's Chief of Personnel. Could die shopping in Tiffany. Wants to remind the motor industry that woman drive too. Likens herself to a retro Roberts radio covered in turquoise Connolly leather. Wishes she could have lived in Restoration London and that Christopher Wren could have built her a house. Fantasy cover story: Vogue,

'Pure style.'

DESIGNER: JOANNA WOOD
COMPANY: JOANNA TRADING, LONDON, ENGLAND

'I BECAME A DESIGNER SO THAT I COULD ALWAYS CREATE A COMFORTABLE HOME'

'MY DESIGN PHILOSOPHY IS REALLY NOT TO HAVE ONE'

Zeynep Fadillioglu

DESIGNER: ZEYNEP FADILLIOGLU
COMPANY: ZF DESIGN, ISTANBUL, TURKEY

Projects: High end residential, offices, restaurants, clubs and shops around Europe

Would have loved to have seen Cleopatra meeting Ceasar as he unrolled her carpet. Was once a computer programmer and systems analyst. Thinks that Guinevere in Chelsea is the most elegant of antique shops. Fancies being Prime Minister or Wonder Woman, to make changes for a much better world. Will be buried on the banks of the Bosphorus.

Fantasy cover story: Time, 'For works on world peace.'

**DESIGNER: VICTORIA KOLOS
COMPANY: KOLOS & KOZYR INTERIORS &
ARCHITECTURE, MOSCOW, RUSSIA**

a kolos

**Projects: Apartments in
Moscow & country houses**

Wanted to be a dancer. Could die shopping in Chantal Thomas' lingerie boutique in Paris. Would love to do an apartment for Björk. Thinks cars should run on lemonade. Is a bit like a kaleidoscope. People watching is better than TV. Plans to be buried in Yalta, on the Black Sea, where she spent her childhood summers.

FANTASY COVER STORY: VOGUE 'THE MOST BEAUTIFUL & TALENTED GIRL IN THE WORLD'

DON'T COLLECT ANYTHING AS ANY COLLECTION

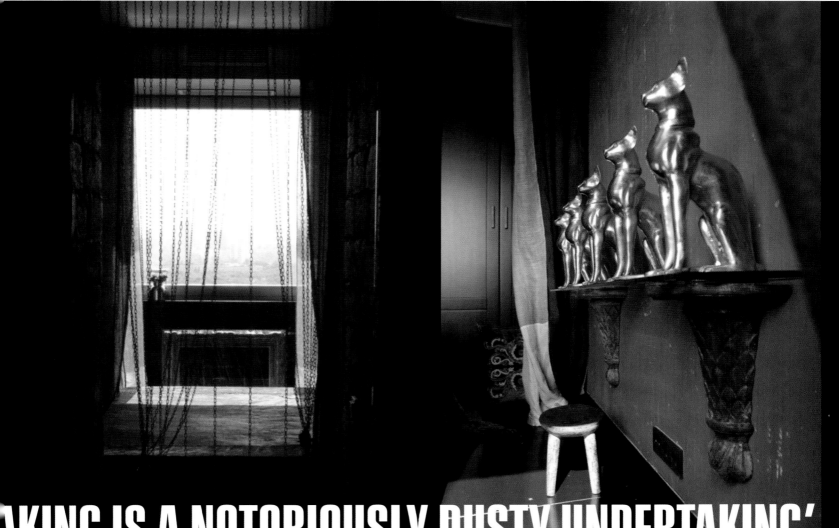

'...AKING IS A NOTORIOUSLY DUSTY UNDERTAKING'

Projects: High-end residences across New England

hilip
van

d in France in the 1930's.

best TV show. Would love to

Fragonard's The Progress of

o be Harry Potter. Dreams of

-Charles Moreux pavilion

m Paris to the hills of

ecticut. And of having a party

l's garden at Munstead Wood

Vould like to be interred at Le

re-Lachaise in Paris for the

ny.

ry: Time,

DESIGNER: PHILIP GORRIVAN
COMPANY: PHILIP GORRIVAN DESIGN, NEW YORK, USA

'THE IDEAL ROOM IS ONE THAT IS FULL OF CONTRASTS TAILORED AND ABOVE ALL VERY COMFORTABLE'

DESIGNER: STEFANO DORATA
COMPANY: STEFANO DORATA ARCHITETTO, ROME, ITALY

Projects: Houses, villas and hotels in Italy, France, Britain, the Middle East, North and South America

'IT'S CRUCIAL THAT MY END DESIGNS CREATE AN EMOTIONAL RESPONSE'

Would have liked to have been a plastic surgeon

Cigarettes should never have been invented

The pencil is the most important invention

Keen to play Marlon Brando's role in Last Tango in Paris

Would fill an empty house with just a piano

Doesn't like collections

Fantasy cover story: Architectural Digest, 'An architect'

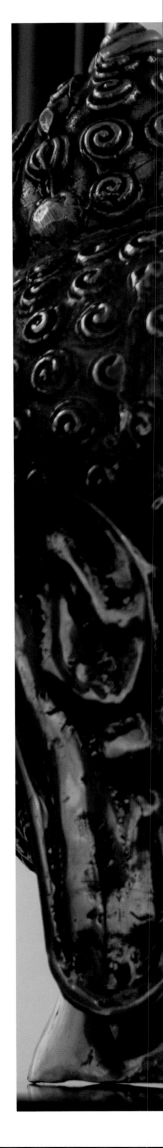

Helen Bygraves & Jenny Weiss

HILL HOUSE

INTERIORS

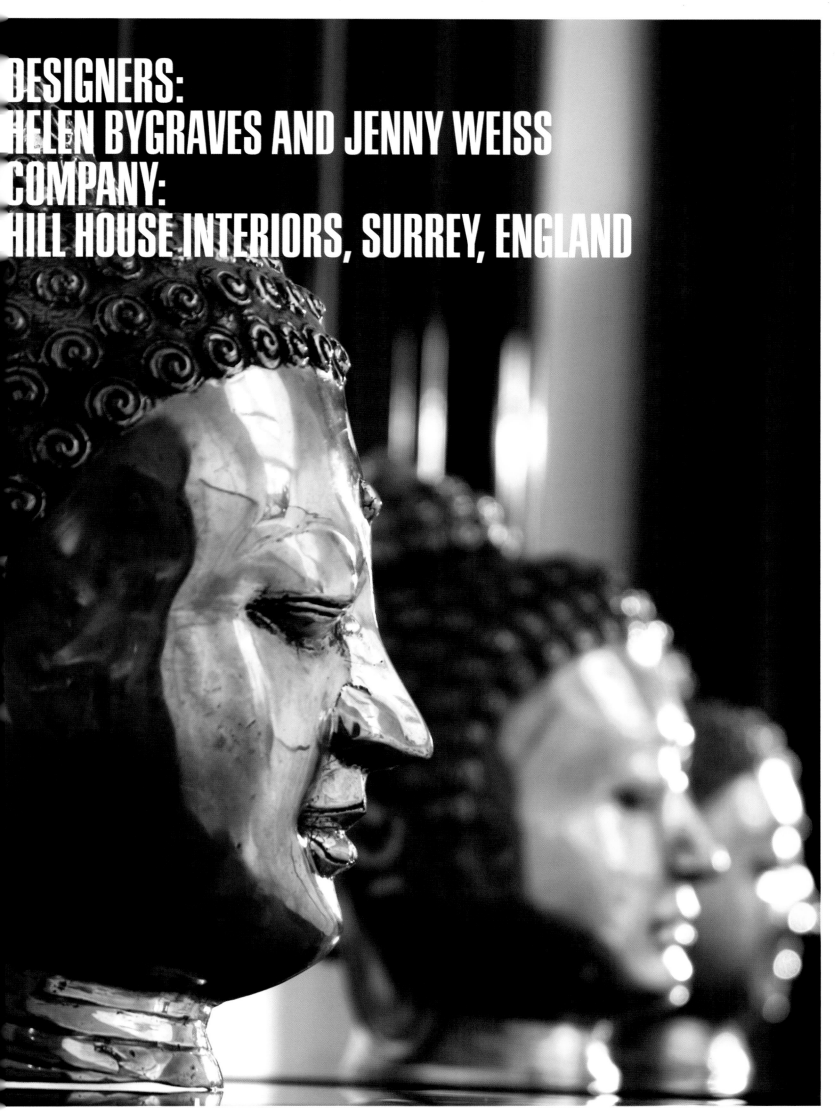

DESIGNERS:
HELEN BYGRAVES AND JENNY WEISS
COMPANY:
HILL HOUSE INTERIORS, SURREY, ENGLAND

Projects:
Contemporary
residences for
city professionals
or modern
families

Both would love to live with ocean views. Helen would commission architect Tony Taylor of Octagon to build her a dream house on the Costa Smerelda, Sardinia. Jenny would have Palladio build her one in the hills overlooking Lake Como. If she had to choose only one colour, Jenny would go with European White. Helen would pick all five shades of Paint Library's Stone. Helen wants to have a party by the pool of the Prince Maurice Hotel in Mauritius. Jenny's would be in the Roof Terrace Bar of the Arabian Court, Royal Mirage in Dubai. Fantasy cover stories: Jenny Weiss - Golf Monthly, 'To see the look on the face of my husband.' Helen Bygraves - Elle Decoration, 'Dynamic duo win top design award.'

Laura O

DESIGNER: LAURA OCAMPO
COMPANY: LAURA OCAMPO & ASSOCIATES,
BUENOS AIRES, ARGENTINA

campo

Projects: Houses, apartments, offices and country homes, as well as art installations

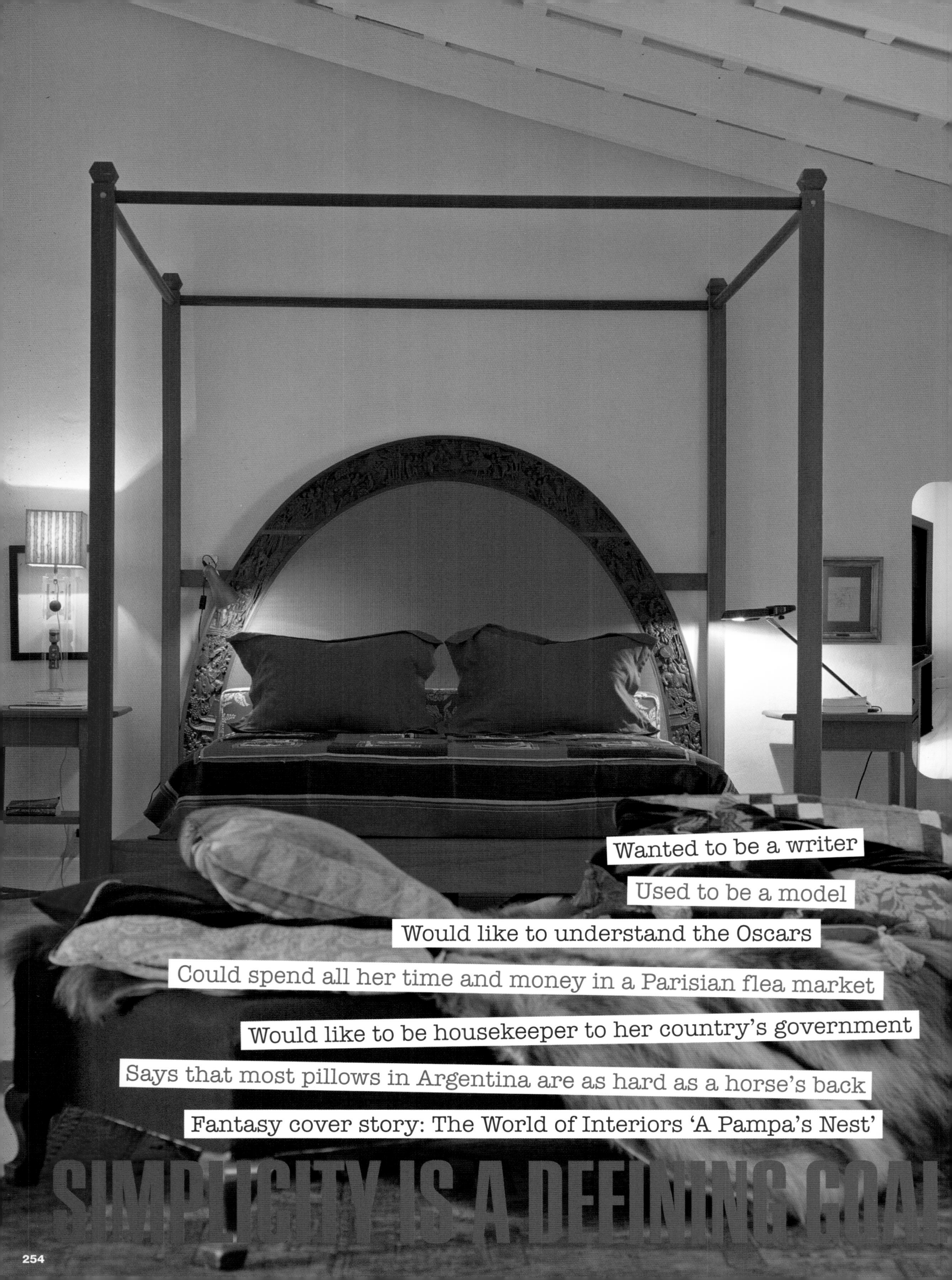

Wanted to be a writer

Used to be a model

Would like to understand the Oscars

Could spend all her time and money in a Parisian flea market

Would like to be housekeeper to her country's government

Says that most pillows in Argentina are as hard as a horse's back

Fantasy cover story: The World of Interiors 'A Pampa's Nest'

SIMPLICITY IS A DEFINING GOAL

'WHAT MOVES ME IS A RESPECT FOR THE PAST – A NEED TO RESTORE THE NEGLECTED AND UNWANTED'

Projects:
Contemporary waterside loft apartments in London and Birmingham, period town and country restorations, retail developments, commercial headquarters and exclusive sports clubs

John Evans

Designer: John Evans. Company: John Evans Interior Architecture and Design, Birmingham, England. Would like to do a post-grad at the RCA. Believes that wine is man's most influential invention.Would like to work in Venice and holiday in Provence. And John Pawson to design his dream house in France. Adores the Hotel Costes in Paris.

Fantasy cover story: Icon,

'Designs for Gucci.'

'I'D SAY MY CURRENT STYLE IS REDEFINED MODERN CLASSIC, WHILE THE FUTURE TREND IS FOR NEW BAROQUE'

Projects: Private residences, embassies and banks

Pedro Guimaraes

Designer: Pedro Guimaraes. Company: PG Design, Porto, Portugal. Could die shopping at River City, Bangkok. Wishes communism had never been thought of. Thinks cars should be covered in coloured rubber. And David Hockney should do his portrait. Collects jade.

Fantasy cover story:

New York Times Magazine,

'PG, the master of colours.'

'I LOVE THE

ENT AND THE ORIENTAL'

DESIGNER: BROOSK SAIB
COMPANY: BROOSK SAIB, LONDON, ENGLAND

Projects: High-end private residences in the UK and abroad

k Saib

'MY MISSION IS TO AMUSE AND ENTERTAIN'

Fantasy cover story: Time

'The world's peacemaker'

Is punctual

Wishes he'd witnessed Napoleon's coronation

Loathes mobile phones - wishes we'd never invented them

Covets a Canaletto of London

Considering moving to Marrakesh

Jaana

Volanen

DESIGNER: JAANA VOLANEN
COMPANY: ART & DESIGN FACTORY, HELSINKI, FINLAND

Projects: Restaurants, clubs, hotels & private residences throughout Finland

FANTASY COVER STORY: VOGUE 'THE MOST STYLISH WOMAN IN THE WORLD'

Could buy everything she ever wanted from the Dolce & Gabbana store in Rome

Would love to work for Manolo Blahnik

Would have loved to have been Snow White

Itching to take Jude Law clubbing to Studio 51 in Helsinki

Emergency packing would comprise her curling tongs, make up and purse

'I'M REALLY INTO DARK, HEAVY OPULENCE AT THE MOMENT – SORT OF A BAROQUE MODERNITY'

STUDIO 51

Projects: High-end urban apartments in new residential developments

Christopher Dezille

Wants to go to Benetton's research school Fabrica in Italy. Admits that he is like a Ragen Synchronar 2100 wrist watch: 'programmed for 100 years, but doesn't keep time.' Would love to be Gene Kelly in Singin' In The Rain. Wants Julian Opie to paint his portrait. Wishes he could have worked with Charles and Ray Eames. Will be buried in a wood covered with bluebells. Could live with just an Arne Jacobsen Egg chair.

Fantasy cover story: Vogue,

'Most wanted.'

DESIGNER: CHRISTOPHER DEZILLE
COMPANY: HONKY DESIGN, LONDON, ENGLAND

'FARROW & BALL'S HARDWICK WHITE IS THE MOST BEAUTIFUL WARM GREY; EVERYTHING YOU SIT WITH IT LOOKS AMAZING'

'I PRIDE MYSELF ON DELIVERING DESIGNS THAT ARE ASPIRATIONAL, WHILE REFLECTING PERSONALITY'

Projects: Up-scale residences, both town and country across Spain

Ana Ros

Designer: Ana Ros. Company: Ana Ros Interior Design, Barcelona, Spain. Compares herself to an empire chandelier. Dreams of being Scarlett O'Hara in Gone with the Wind. Is precious about her Limoges crockery. Her dream home is built by Palladio on a Greek island with sea views. But Michael Douglas' house on Mallorca would do just fine.

Fantasy cover story: Architectural Digest, 'My best work.'

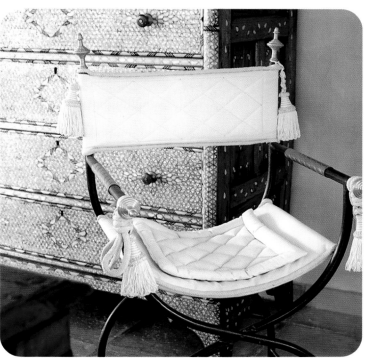

Jan
Wilson

Designer: Jan Wilson. Company: RPW Design, London, England. Dreams of going up to Cambridge to read science and humanities. Could spend a fortune in any of the better UK estate agencies. Wishes she had been a man in late eighteenth century England. John Singer Seargent was the most brilliant portrait artist. Loves the Sussex Downs, the Wallace Collection and Cumbria. But would like to live and work in Sydney. Collects Christmas decorations. Would like to have a party in the Sir John Soane Museum.

FANTASY COVER STORY: THE ECONOMIST 'THE ALCHEMIST OF HOTEL DESIGN'

LIFESTYLES

South

DESIGNER: JOHN HUNTER
COMPANY: LIFESTYLES INTERIORS,
LONDON, ENGLAND

INTERIORS

Projects: Contemporary high end residential, including
houses, apartments and show homes in refurbished

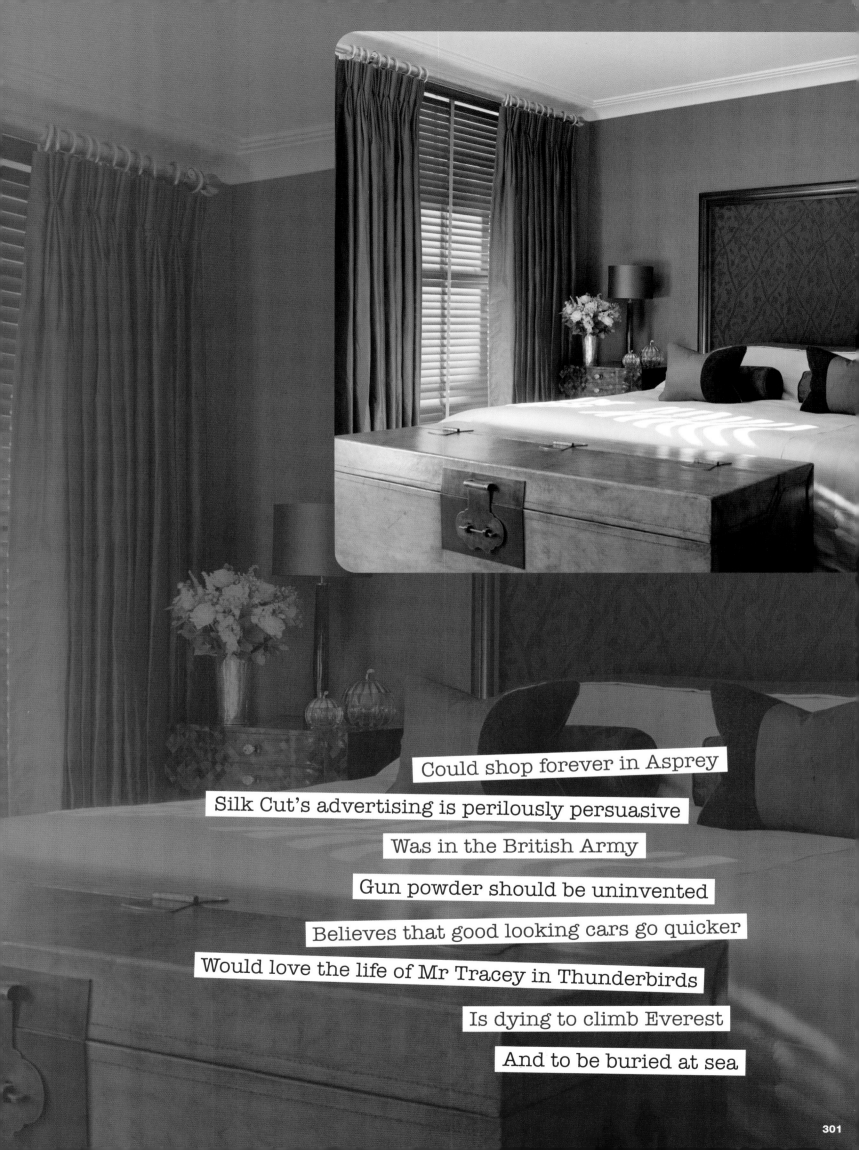

Could shop forever in Asprey

Silk Cut's advertising is perilously persuasive

Was in the British Army

Gun powder should be uninvented

Believes that good looking cars go quicker

Would love the life of Mr Tracey in Thunderbirds

Is dying to climb Everest

And to be buried at sea

FANTASY COVER STORY: FORBES 'THE NEW DONALD TRUMP'

Projects:
Contemporary residences, clubs and hotels plus private ships across Europe, Scandinavia and the US

William Cummings

Designer: William Cummings.

Company: Heiberg Cummings Design, NYC, USA. Would like to be painted by Rembrandt. Wants the Dalai Lama's number. And to live the life of Dorian Gray. Or to visit Sumatra. And a bedroom on Mykonos with a sea view. Hopes to be buried in Storm King Park, Upstate NY.

Fantasy cover story:

New York Times Magazine,

'Top of the Wave.'

'HISTORY AND ORNAMENT
ARE WELL AND TRULY BACK'

'A HOUSE WITHOUT A VIEW IS JUST AWFUL'

Helene

Hennie

Projects: Residences, vacation homes, restaurants and hotels in Scandinavia and Europe

DESIGNER: HELENE FORBES HENNIE
COMPANY: HENNIE INTERIORS, OSLO, NORWAY

FANTASY COVER STORY:
TATLER
'MOTHER OF THE YEAR'

Has never considered being anything other than an interior designer

Would shop till her plastic melted in Donna Karen, New York

Would like to see the designs of the 1980s uninvented

Knows that less is always more and sticks to it

Dream house would be designed by Frank Lloyd Wright
overlooking the ocean

The Kennedy compound on Martha's vineyard would be her holiday home

'OUR DESIGN CONCEPT IS CLASSICAL MODERN WITH CLEAN AND TIMELESS LINES, COMBINED WITH SOFTNESS THROUGH THE USE OF FABRICS AND TEXTURES'

FEDERICA

DESIGNER: FEDERICA PALACIOS COMPANY: FEDERICA PALACIOS DESIGN, GENEVA, SWITZERLAND

Projects: Luxury private residences around Western Europe

PALACIOS

Has never interviewed for a job. Would work for Tom Ford, designing furniture. Would love to get her parents an executive chief assistant. Wishes she had lived in Renaissance Florence. And sat for Andy Warhol. Wants to be buried by her children's chalet in the Swiss Alps.

FANTASY COVER STORY: ARCHITECTURAL DIGEST 'TIMELESS DESIGN'

I like to be influenced by the client if they have a lot of personality

Projects:
Exclusive private residences, luxury hotels, company headquarters and casinos

Tessa Kennedy

Designer: Tessa Kennedy. Company: Tessa Kennedy Design, London, England. She and her sister were the first twins to fly across the Atlantic. Wanted to be an actress. Or mistress to Louis XIV. Has got almost everyone's number. Took Mike Tyson to the Louvre. Wants to live in a William Burgess gothic castle.

Fantasy cover story: Vanity Fair,

'Friend and decorator to the stars.'

BIBIS CRITERION RESTAURANT LEEDS : BEFORE IMAGES OF THE GROUND FLOOR OF A NEW CAR PARK

PHOTO'S, IMAGES & INSPIRATION OF THE COMPLETED PROJECT

'ALTHOUGH OUR OFFICE USES COMPUTER DRAWINGS VIRTUALLY ALL THE TIME, I REALLY PREFER THE HAND DRAWN SKETCHES AND VISUALS'

Projects: Restaurants, hotels, offices, cruise ships and the QM2

Andrew Collier

Designer: Andrew Collier. Company: SMC Design, London, England. Dying to see an active volcano in Hawaii. Would love Michael Caine's role in The Italian Job, 'great style, great suits and great lines.' Fawlty Towers is the best television show ever. Loves JMW Turner's Fighting Termeraire for its great sense of space and light. Wants the indomitable Frank Lloyd Wright to design and build him a house in Southern England, on a Capability Brown rolling landscape with deer park, follies and ornamental lake.

Fantasy cover story: Anglers Mail,

'New world record holder for a rod caught Blue Marlin.'

'I HAVE THE BEST JOB IN THE WORLD NOW, SO WHY SHOULD I WANT TO WORK FOR ANYBODY ELSE?'

Projects: Luxury residential apartments, houses and hotels around the world

Françoise de Pfyffer

Designer: Françoise de Pfyffer. Company: Françoise de Pfyffer Interior Design, Geneva, Switzerland. Fancied being an opera singer. Wishes she could have designed the Hermes H. Collects antique boxes and old bottles. Covets a collection of Mark Rothko paintings. Would like to star in a Franco Zeffirelli film. Her dream home would overlook the Mediterranean Sea and be designed by Frank Lloyd Wright, with a waterfall behind which would run under the house and be seen through floors of glass. Bought bronze furniture direct from Diego Giacometti.

Monika

DESIGNER: MONIKA APPONYI
COMPANY: MM DESIGN, LONDON, ENGLAND

Projects: Luxury residences in
Europe & America, as well as hotels,
golf clubs and banks

'SOME THINGS GET BETTER WITH AGE'

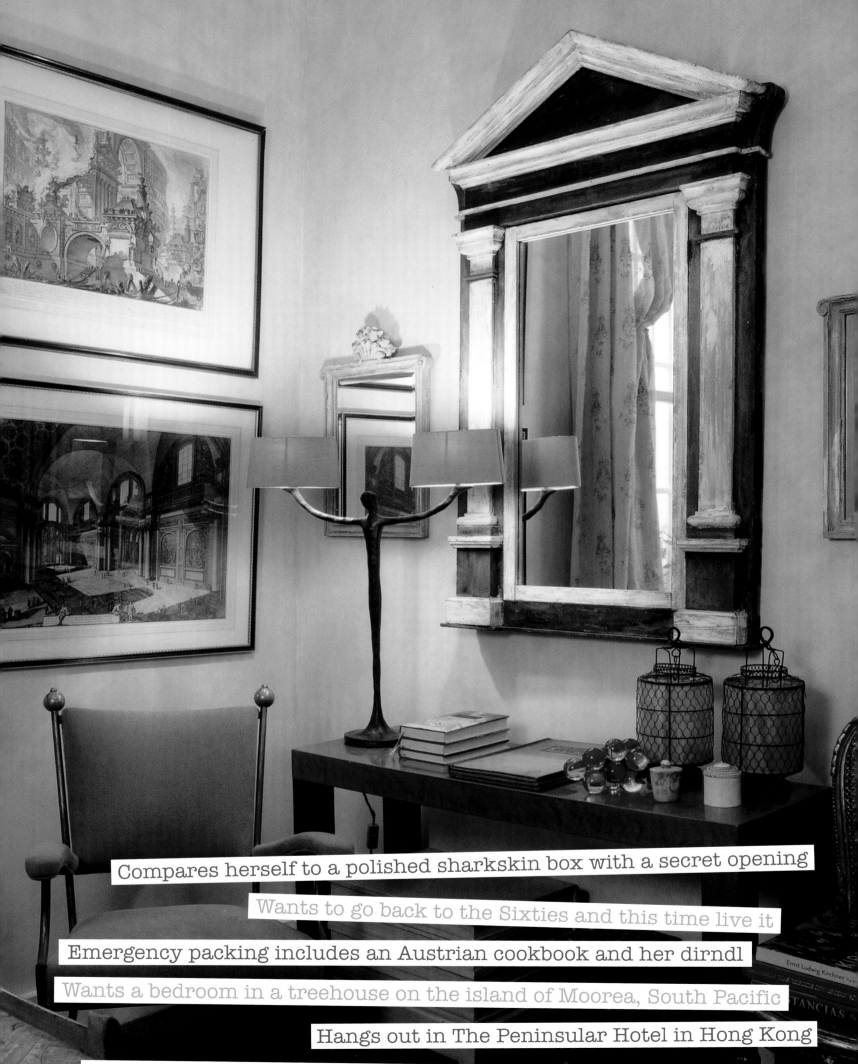

Compares herself to a polished sharkskin box with a secret opening

Wants to go back to the Sixties and this time live it

Emergency packing includes an Austrian cookbook and her dirndl

Wants a bedroom in a treehouse on the island of Moorea, South Pacific

Hangs out in The Peninsular Hotel in Hong Kong

Fantasy Cover Story: The world of Interiors 'The best is yet to come'

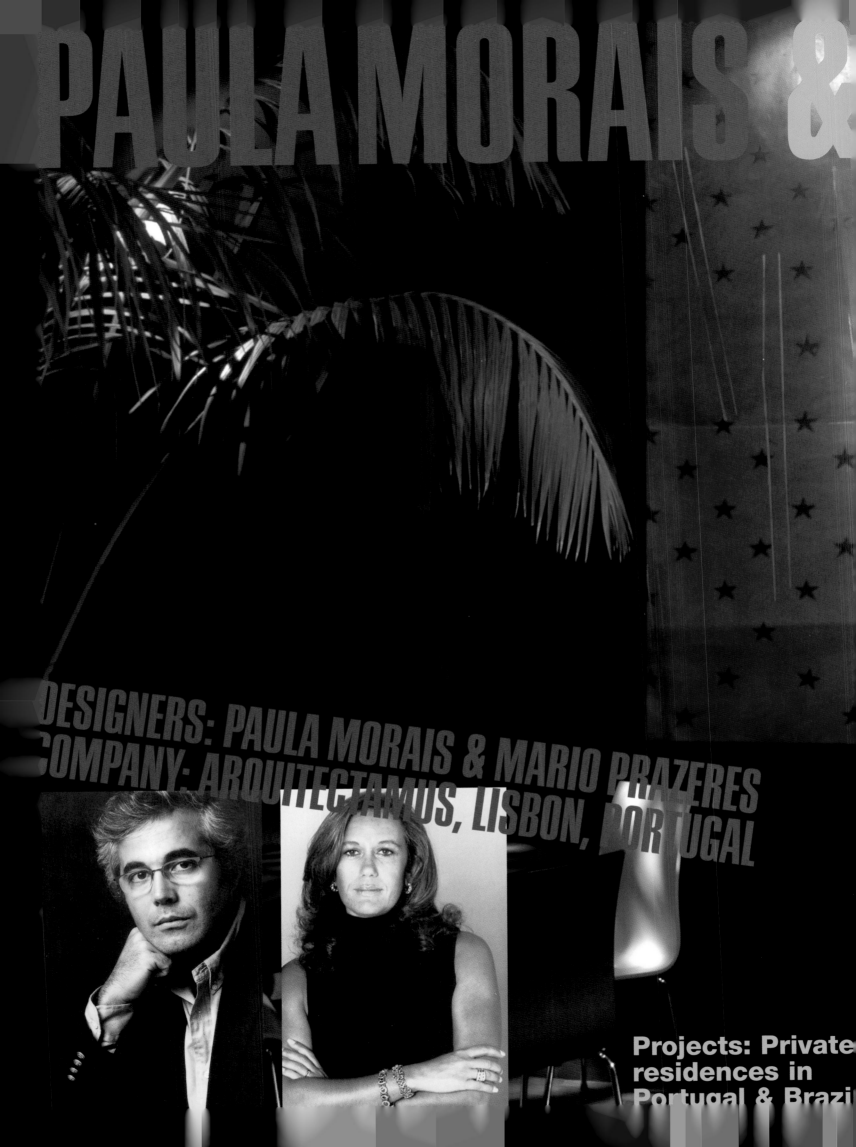

PAULA MORAIS &

DESIGNERS: PAULA MORAIS & MARIO PRAZERES
COMPANY: ARQUITECTAMUS, LISBON, PORTUGAL

Projects: Private
residences in
Portugal & Brazil

'WE LOVE DARK, INKY PALETTES'

Falls asleep in front of the television

Would like to be more like James Bond

Or Louis XV's treasury minister

Love and want the work of Vieira da Silva

Have a house in old Evora

And would like one on an island in the Indian Ocean

351

FANTASY COVER STORY: TIME 'THE GREATES

Projects: Contemporary luxury residences, commercial property and hotels around the world

Martin Hulbert

Designer: Martin Hulbert. Company: Fox Linton Associates, London, England. Wishes there was no prejudice against modernism. And that the motor industry should go green. Is keen to see the sights of Samarkand. And to die looking at a starry sky or full moon. Then be buried in a beechwood.

Fantasy cover story: National Enquirer, 'Alien arrives in New York.'

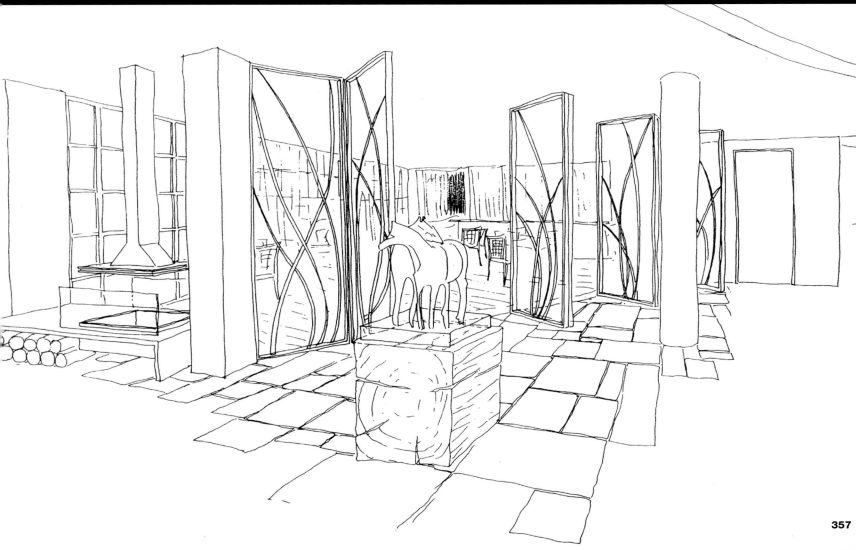

'IF ONLY THE VICTORIA & ALBERT MUSEUM WERE A STORE'

Homeira Pour Heidari

DESIGNER:
HOMEIRA POUR HEIDARI
COMPANY:
HOMEIRA ARCHITECTURAL
DESIGN/INTERIOR DESIGN
MUNICH, GERMANY

Projects: High end private residences and some commercial property in Germany, Switzerland, England and America

Wants to be an Academy member that gets to vote the Oscars

Adores Bergdorf Goodman in New York

Loathes Birkenstock shoes and wishes they have never been thought of

Would be carved in solid marble by Michelangelo

And desires to own his Pieta

Happy to have a working home in London

And a play one in South Africa

'MY STYLE IS MULTI-CULTURAL AND BEYOND THE BOUNDARIES OF TIME'

FANTASY COVER STORY: TIME MAGAZINE 'THE WHITE HOUSE HAS BEEN REDESIGNED'

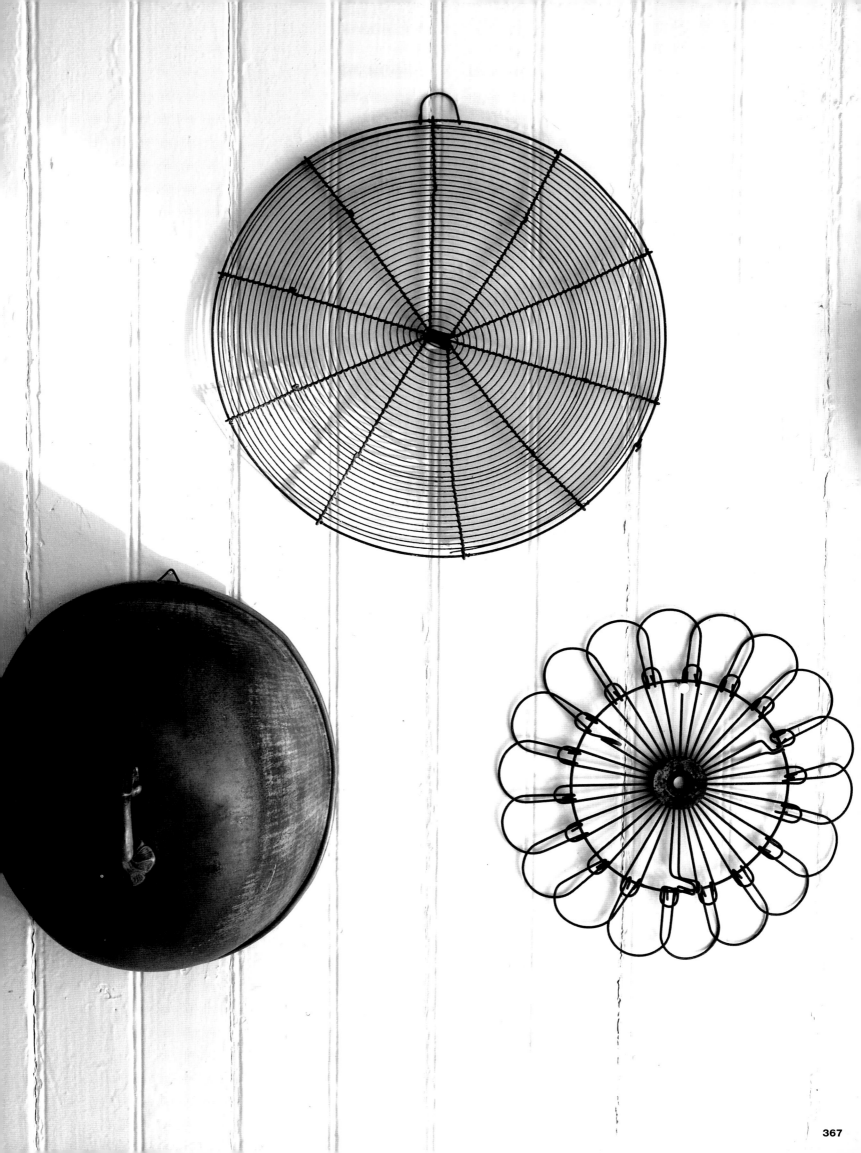

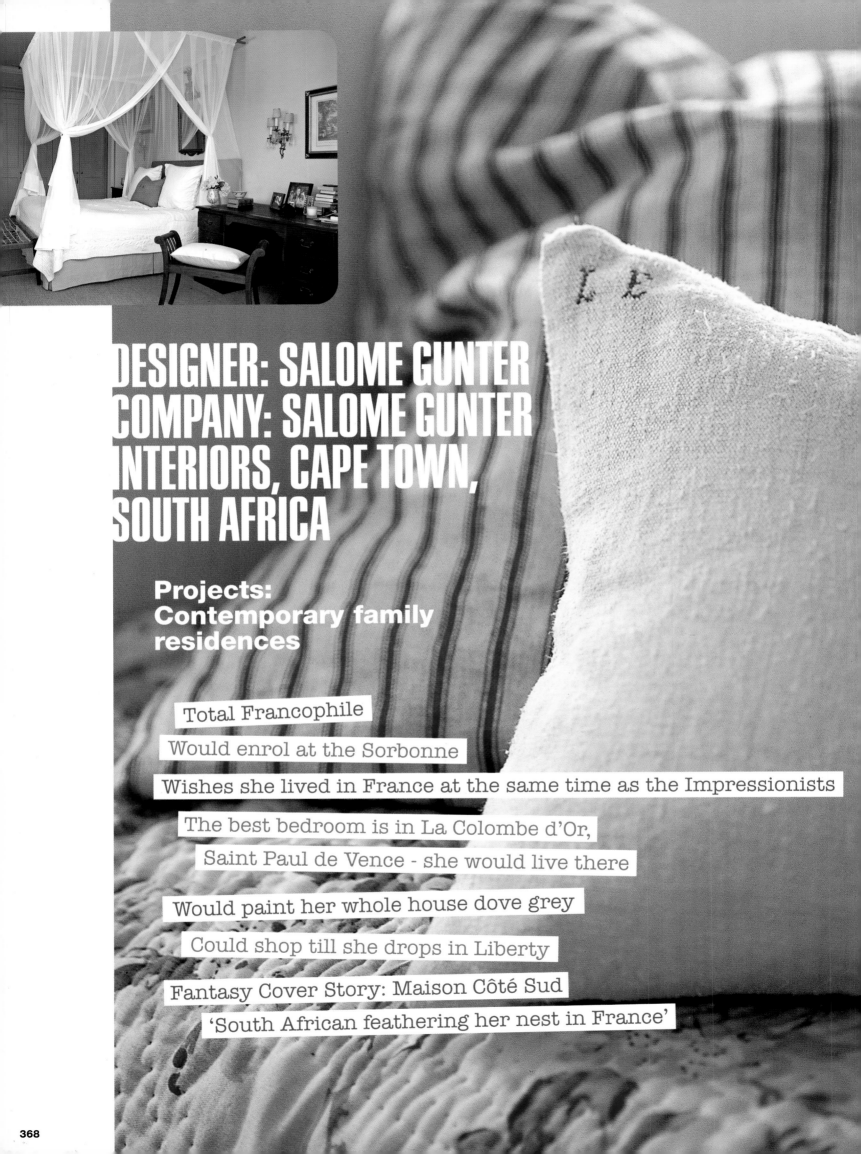

DESIGNER: SALOME GUNTER
COMPANY: SALOME GUNTER INTERIORS, CAPE TOWN, SOUTH AFRICA

Projects: Contemporary family residences

Total Francophile

Would enrol at the Sorbonne

Wishes she lived in France at the same time as the Impressionists

The best bedroom is in La Colombe d'Or, Saint Paul de Vence - she would live there

Would paint her whole house dove grey

Could shop till she drops in Liberty

Fantasy Cover Story: Maison Côté Sud

'South African feathering her nest in France'

Projects:
Luxury goods retail outlets, restaurants and high-end residences in Brazil and Portugal

Joáo Mansur

Designer: Joáo Mansur. Company: Joáo Mansur Architecture & Design, Sao Paulo, Brazil. Would like to study at the Milan School of Industrial Design. Could happily bid forever in Sotheby's, London. Loves Levi's ad campaigns. Would like to live the life of da Vinci. Could have his whole home a light tone of chocolate.

Gail Taylor &

Projects: Primarily residential, including show apartments, health spas, hotels and offices

DESIGNERS: GAIL TAYLOR & KAREN HOWES
COMPANY: TAYLOR HOWES DESIGNS,
LONDON, ENGLAND

Karen Howes

Gail would love to be a musician, Karen a geologist

Karen wants to join the China Club in Hong Kong

Gail the Electric in Notting Hill

Both love Beanz Meanz Heinz slogan

Gail wants a view of uninterrupted English countryside

Karen wants rolling Tuscan hills

Fantasy cover story: Tatler, 'Fabulous at forty.'

Telephone tales: Gail to Brad Pitt: 'How about dinner?'

Karen to George Clooney: 'Would you like to join Gail, Brad and I for dinner?'

'AT EVERY TURN
THERE SHOULD BE
SOMETHING BOLD
AND DIFFERENT
TO EXCITE'

Directory of Designers

4 Tara Bernerd
Target Living
6A Pont Street, London SW1X 9EL
Tel 0207 823 2316
Fax 0207 823 2317
tara@targetliving.com

14 Vicente Wolf
Vicente Wolf Associates, Inc.
333 West 39th Street, Suite 1001
New York, NY 10018, U.S.A.
Tel 001 212 465 0590
Fax 001 212 465 0639
Vicente.wolf@verizon.net

18 Jorge Fuentes
Estudio F
C/Maestro Perez Cabrero no. 3
08021 Barcelona, Spain.
Tel 0034 93 241 1038
Fax 0034 93 202 1167

24 Nicky Dobree
Nicky Dobree Interior Design Ltd.
25 Lansdowne Gardens
London SW8 2EQ
Tel 0207 627 0469
Fax 0207 627 0469
info@nickydobree.com

28 Alexandra Champalimaud
Alexandra Champalimaud
& Associates
One, Union Square West,
Suite 603, New York,
New York 10003.
Tel 001 212 807 8869
Fax 001 212 807 1742
anthonyc@alexchamp.com

36 Irina Dymova
30/12, Shabolovka Str,
Apartment 114,
Moscow 117319, Russia.
Tel 007 095 236 4190
Fax 007 095 953 9863
Mobile 007 095 729 0730
unistts@yahoo.com

42 Kit Kemp
18 Thurloe Place,
London SW7 2SP
Tel 0207 581 4045
Fax 0207 581 1867
kitkemp@firmdale.com

50 Mr Joseph Sy
Joseph Sy and Associates
17th Fl. Heng Shan Centre
145 Queen's Road East
Wanchai, Hong Kong.
Tel: 00 852 2866 1333
Fax: 00 852 2866 1222
joseph@jsahk.com
www.jsahk.com

56 Jan des Bouvrie
Studio Het Arsenaal B.V.
Kooltjesbuurt 1, 1411 RZ Naarden
The Netherlands
Tel 0031 (0) 35 6996 200
Fax 0031 (0) 35 6310 100
info@hetarsenaal.nl
www.hetarsenaal.nl

62 Rabih Hage
Rabih Hage Ltd.
69-71 Sloane Avenue
London SW3 3DH
Tel 0207 823 8288
Fax 0207 823 8258
info@rabih-hage.com

68 Marc Hertrich & Nicolas Adnet
Studio Marc Hertrich
15 rue Gambey, 75011, Paris.
Tel 00 331 43 14 00 00
Fax 00 331 43 14 00 22
contact@marchertrich.com
wwww.marchertrich.com

74 Silvio Rech & Lesley Carstens
Architecture and Interior Design
32B Pallinghurst Road, Westcliff,
Johannesburg, 2193,
South Africa.
Tel/fax 0027 11 486 1525
Mobile 0027 82 900 9935
adventarch@mweb.co.za

80 Frederick Sutherland
Frederick Sutherland & Co.
712 Woodlawn Avenue
Venice Ca 90291, U.S.A.
Tel 001 310 652 3733
Fax 001 310 578 9669
www.fredericksutherland.com

86 Artistic Design
Spiridonovka Stra. 9/2,
Office 070, 123001, Moscow,
Russia.
Tel 007 095 203 3397
Fax 007 095 203 5642
dvelikovsky@co.ru
iageeva@co.ru

90 Sara A. Al-Faisal
Alssamoure Design Associates
P.O. Box 15707, Riyadh 11454
Saudi Arabia.
Tel 00966 1 441 2723/441 2746
Fax 00966 1 441 2651
simals@simals.com

94 Sue Rohrer
Sue Rohrer Zumikon SA
Chapfstrasse 106
8126 Zumikon, Switzerland.
Tel 0041 44 919 0290
Fax 0041 44 919 0288
suerohrer@bluewin.ch
www.suerohrer.com

98 Laura Carter
& Patrick Tyberghein
CarterTyberghein
Hyde Park House,
Manfred Road, London SW15 2RS.
Tel 0208 871 4800
Fax 0208 871 4900
info@cartertyberghein.com

104 Peter Nolden
Peter Interior Design
Isestrasse 84,
20149 Hamburg,
Germany.
Tel 0049 40 482 509
Fax 0049 40 482 509
info@peter-interior.de
www.peter-interior.de

108 Scott Sanders
Scott Sanders LLC
524 Broadway, Suite 400A
New York, NY 10012
Tel 001 212 343 8298
Fax 001 212 343 8299
scott@scottsandersllc.com
www. scottsandersllc.com

114 Jane Churchill
Jane Churchill Interiors
81 Pimlico Road
London SW1W 8PH
Tel 0207 730 8564
Fax 0207 823 6421
jchurchill@janechurchillinteriors.co.uk
www.janechurchillinteriors.com

120 Nadya & Georgy Ananiev
Novopeschanaya str. 24-38
Moscow, Russia 125252
Tel 007 095 198 04 37
Fax 007 095 978 38 92
givi@formatek.ru

126 David Lees
David Lees Productions, Inc.
511, 6th Avenue, #17A New York,
New York, 10011, U.S.A.
Mobile: 001 917 887 0045
Office: 001 212 629 4321
Fax: 001 212 268 3524
david@davidleesproductions.com
www.davidleesproductions.com

130 Osca and Pierrette Reuchlin
GR Home – Georgette Reuchlin
Kerkplein 12, 2061 JD
Bloemendaal, Holland.
Tel 0031 235 275 308
Fax 0031 235 272 502
grhome@planet.nl

136 Seyhan Özdemir-Sefer Çaglar
Autoban Design Studio
Architectural, Interior, Product
Tatarbey s. No 1\2 Galata,
Istanbul, Turkey.
Tel 00 90 212 243 86 41
Fax 00 90 212 243 86 40
info@autoban212.com
www.autoban212.com

142 François Champsaur
Agence Francois Champsaur
56 rue du Faubourg Saint Antoine
Cour du Bel Air
75012, Paris, France.
Tel 0033 1 4345 2246
Fax 0033 1 4345 2256
agence@champsaur.com
www.champsaur.com

148 Debbie Hindman
Associates 111
1516 Blake Street, Denver
Co 80202, U.S.A.
Tel 001 303 534 4444
Fax 001 303 629 9035
Debbie@associates3.com
www.associates3.com

152 Angelos Angelopoulos
Angelos Angelopoulos
5 Proairesiou St
11636 Athens, Greece.
Tel 0030 210 756 7191
Fax 0030 210 756 7191
agelosad@otenet.gr

158 Law Ling Kit & Virginia Lung
One Plus Partnership Limited
16A, 332 Lockhart Road,
Wanchai, Hong Kong.
Tel 852 259 19308
Fax 852 259 19362
admin@onepluspartnership.com

164 Howard Pharr
Hirsch Bedner Associates
909 West Peachtree St. N.E.
Atlanta, Georgia.
30309-3839 USA
Tel 001 404 873 4379
Fax 001 404 872 3588
and
Michael Bedner
Hirsch Bedner Associates
3216 Nebraska Avenue
Santa Monica, California
90404 U.S.A.
Tel 001 310 829 9087
Fax 001 310 453 1182

170 Azul Tierra & Toni Espuch
Azul Tierra
C/Corcega no 302
08008 Barcelona, Spain.
Tel 0034 932 178 356
Fax 0034 932 384 946
and
Azul Tierra
C/Angel Lozano no 2
03001 Alicante, Spain.
Tel 0034 965 2083 40
Fax 0034 965 1402 03
azultierra@azultierra.es

176 Helen Green
Helen Green Design
6 Burnsall Street
London SW3 3ST
Tel 0207 352 3344
Fax 0207 352 5544
mail@helengreendesign.com
www.helengreendesign.com

180 Alessandra Branca
Branca
1325 N. State Parkway
Chicago, IL 60610, U.S.A.
Tel 001 312 787 6123
Fax 001 312 787 6125
abranca@branca.com

188 Ernest de la Torre
de la Torre design studio, ltd.
526 West 26th Street, Suite 6AA,
NY, NY 10001, U.S.A.
Tel 001 212 243 5202
Fax 001 212 243 5582
ernest@delatorredesign.com

194 Dickie Bannenberg
Bannenberg Designs
6 Burnsall Street,
London SW3 3ST.
Tel +44 (0) 207 352 4851
Fax +44 (0) 207 352 8444
yachts@bannenberg.com
www.bannenberg.com

202 Steve C. T. Leung
Steve Leung Designers Ltd.
9/F, Block C, Sea View Estate,
8 Watson Road, North Point,
Hong Kong.
Tel 00 852 2527 1600
Fax 00 852 2527 2071
steve@steveleung.com.hk
www.steveleung.com

208 Brian Gluckstein
Gluckstein Design Planning Inc.
234 Davenport Road, Toronto,
Ontario, M5R 1J6.
Tel 001 416 928 2067
Fax 001 928 2114
briang@glucksteindesign.com

214 Ricardas Vysniauskas
Ricardas Vysniauskas
Traidenio 31-1, Vilnius,
Lithuania 2004.
Tel 0037 052 610 696
Fax 0037 052 120 459
Mobile 0037 065 047 862
Vysnia.arch@parkas.lt

222 Joanna Wood
Joanna Trading Ltd
7 Bunhouse Place
London SW1W 8HU
Tel 0207 730 0693
Fax 0207 730 4135
joannaw@joannawood.com

228 Zeynep Fadillioglu
ZF Design, Ahmet Adnan
Saygun Caddesi Dag
Apt. 72/5 Ulus
Istanbul 34340, Turkey.
Tel 0090 212 287 0936
Fax 0090 212 287 0994
design@zfdesign.com

232 Victoria Kolos & Alexei Kozyr
1 Kudrinskaya Square,
Apartment 99,
Moscow 121069, Russia.
Tel 007 095 797 5631
Fax 007 095 783 3601
office@arch4.ru
www.arch4.ru

238 Philip Gorrivan
Philip Gorrivan Design
155a East 71st Street
New York, NY 10021, U.S.A.
Tel 001 212 452 1717
Fax 001 212 452 2228
Philip@philipgorrivan.com

242 Stefano Dorata
Stefano Dorata Architetto
00197 Roma, 23 Via Francesco
Denza, Italy.
Tel 0039 06 8084 747
Fax 0039 06 8077 695
studio@stefanodorata.com

246 Helen Bygraves
& Jenny Weiss
Hill House Interiors
Marie House, 5 Baker Street,
Weybridge, Surrey, KT13 8AE
Tel 01932 858 900
Fax 01932 858 997
design@hillhouseinteriors.com
www.hillhouseinteriors.com

252 Laura Ocampo
Laura Ocampo & Associates
Av. Quintana 104,
6th Floor (1014) CP
Capital Federal, Buenos Aires,
Argentina.
Tel 005411 4326 1065
Fax 005411 4747 2462
Mobile 005411 94445 1517
Lola3040@argencorp.com
www.lauraocampo.com

256 John Evans Interior
Architecture & Design Ltd
Victoria Works, 16 Vittoria Street,
Birmingham, B1 3PE.
Tel 0121 233 9041
Fax 0121 233 4641
john@johnevansdesign.com

262 Pedro Guimaraes
Av. Da Boavista 1503
4100-131 Porto
tel/fax 00351 22 609 60 69
mpedroguimaraes@iol.pt

268 Broosk Saib
Broosk Saib, 4 Heathrise,
Kersfield Road,
London SW15 3HF.
Tel 0208 788 5130
Fax 0208 788 5130
broosksaib@aol.com

272 Jaana Volanen
Jaana Volanen Art and Design
Factory OY, Kasarminkatu 14c
00130 Helsinki, Finland.
Tel 00 358 40 839 0749
Fax 00 358 96 229 2333
Jaana.volanen@sk-ravintolat.com

278 Christopher Dezille
Honky Design, The Studio
26A Oakmead Road
London SW12 9SL
Tel 07786 131 186
Fax 0208 672 1765
dizzy@honkydesign.co.uk
www.honkydesign.co.uk

284 Ana Ros
Ana Ros Factory Interior Design
Diputacion 290 - Showroom
08009, Barcelona, Spain.
Tel 0034 93 41 22 534
Fax 0034 93 34 24 563
anarosbcn@eresmas.com
www.anarosbcn.com

290 Jan Wilson
RPW Design
10-13 The Leathermarket
Weston Street, London SE1 3ER
Tel 0207 378 8001
Fax 0207 403 6754
rpw@rpwdesign.com
www.rpwdesign.com

298 Lifestyles Interiors Ltd.
48 Old Church Street
London SW3 5BY
Tel 0207 349 8020
lifestyles@northacre.co.uk

304 William Cummings
& Bernt Heiberg
Heiberg Cummings Design
9 W 19th St # 3f1
New York, NY 10011, U.S.A.
Tel 001 212 337 2030
Fax 001 212 337 2033
wcummings@hcd3.com

and Heiberg Cummings Design
Gimleveien 22
0266 Oslo, Norway
Tel 0047 221 29870
Fax 0047 221 29879
eram@hcd3.com

310 Helene Forbes Hennie
Hennie Interiors
Thomlesgt. 4
0270 Oslo, Norway.
Tel 0047 220 685 86
Fax 0047 220 685 87
helene@hinteriors.no

318 Federica Palacios
Federica Palacios Design
3 Cour St Pierre
Geneva,
Switzerland.
Tel 0041 79 433 1393
Fax 0041 22 310 2286

324 Tessa Kennedy
Tessa Kennedy Design Limited
Studio 5, 2 Olaf Street
London W11 4BE.
Tel 0207 221 4546
Fax 0207 229 2899
info@tessakennedydesign.com

332 Andrew Collier
SMC Design
7-10 Charlotte Mews
London W1T 4EE
Tel 0207 436 6466
Fax 0207 436 6226
andyc@smc-design.com

338 Françoise de Pfyffer
Francoise de Pfyffer
Interior Design
6 rue Eynard,
1205 Geneva,
Switzerland.
Tel 004 122 312 4431/4429
Fax 0044 122 310 0145
f.depfyffer@bluewin.ch

342 Monika Apponyi
MM Design, The Studio,
Redloh House,
2 Michael Rd,
London, SW6 2AD.
Tel + 44 207 751 0171
Fax + 44 207 751 0172
info@mm-design.co.uk

348 Paula Morais/Mario Prazeres
Arquitectamus
Rua da Escola Politecnica
no 231-1 Esq.
1250-101 Lisboa,
Portugal.
Tel 00351 213 872036
Fax 00351 213 872 038
arquitectamus@mail.telepac.PT

354 Martin Hulbert
Fox Linton Associates
4 Hewlett House,
Havelock Terrace
London SW8 4AS
Tel 0207 622 0920
Fax 0207 622 1982
email@foxlinton.co.uk

360 Homeira Pour Heidari
Homeira Pour Heidari
Architectural Design/
Interior Design
Lucile-Grahn-Str. 38
81675 Munich, Germany
Tel: 0049 172 67 27 647
Fax: 0049 894 19 29 407
homeira.design@gmail.com

366 Salome Gunter
Salome Gunter Interiors
2 Beauchamp Place
27 Wolfe Street, Wynberg,
7800 Cape Town,
South Africa.
Tel 0027 21 762 9512
Fax 0027 21 762 9514
wgunter@intekom.co.za

372 Joao Mansur
Joao Mansur Architecture
& Design
1922b, rua Groenlandia,
01434-100, Sao Paulo-SP-Brazil.
Tel 00 5511 3083 1500
Fax 00 5511 3081 7732
joaomansur@joaomansur.com
www.joaomansur.com

376 Gail Taylor & Karen Howes
Taylor Howes Designs Ltd
29 Fernshaw Road
London SW10 OTG
Tel 0207 349 9017
Fax 0207 349 9018
admin@thdesigns.co.uk
www.thdesigns.co.uk